Endorsements

Defining Life by Your Dreams Not Difficulties is a fascinating book! The Gilmours offer a unique perspective into daily spiritual practices and personal growth by sharing their uncanny experiences. As I read this book, I was brought to tears through learning of the death of their daughter and inspired by their downright tenacity to define life by one's dreams and not one's difficulties, as this work is titled. I have been challenged to become a better husband, leader, and Christ follower. I know you will find this book just as moving as I did."

—**Dr. John Braland**
Lead Pastor and founder of FreshWater Community Church
President and General Overseer, International
Ministerial Fellowship
Author, "Wounded to Wonderful"

* * * * * * * * * * * * * *

Defining Life by Your Dreams Not Difficulties is more than an inspirational book; it's a collection of real-life examples of how people like you and me have made unique choices that have changed their lives, as well as the world around them. Hebrews 6:12 says, " …be an imitator of those who through faith and patience inherit the promises." This book will challenge you to be such an imitator."

—**Jeff Scislow**, Eight-time top REMAX Realtor
Minnesota, Author, *Journey to a Miracle—When Faith Was the Only Cure* International speaker/presenter

* * * * * * * * * * * * * *

In my years of pastoring, I've noticed everyone has two things: dreams from God and difficulties from life. Often these things appear to be against each other. George Gilmour's new book gracefully shows how to live out your dreams and get past difficulties. Pick it up, and discover the fulfillment living out your God-given dreams can bring—the best is yet to come!

—**Pastor Rob Ketterling**
Lead pastor, River Valley Church
Author, *Change before You Have To*

* * * * * * * * * * * * * * * *

This book will equip you on your journey through life's struggles and challenges. George and Becky are excellent guides through the desert or wilderness or what seems to be the uncrossable mountains of life.

—**Pastor Blane Huston**
Staff pastor, Mercy Hill Church, Rochester, Minnesota
Recovery Coach, Rochester Adult & Teen Challenge

* * * * * * * * * * * * * * * *

This book encouraged me to continue working on the novel I've been writing for a little over three years. George and Becky, you have my personal thanks! I know this book will be a powerful tool to help many endure pain and move past boredom and unhappiness to personal revival.

—**B. McPherson**, director of operations of
the Salvation Poem Foundation

* * * * * * * * * * * * * * * *

"A highly personal and ultimately uplifting faith manual."

—*Kirkus Reviews*

DEFINING LIFE BY YOUR DREAMS -NOT- DIFFICULTIES

GEORGE & BECKY GILMOUR

WESTBOW
PRESS®
A DIVISION OF THOMAS NELSON
& ZONDERVAN

WestBow Press books may be ordered through booksellers or by contacting:

WestBow Press
A Division of Thomas Nelson & Zondervan
1663 Liberty Drive
Bloomington, IN 47403
www.westbowpress.com
844-714-3454

Photos and cover design by Gilmour Creative.

ISBN: 978-1-5127-0786-1 (sc)
ISBN: 978-1-5127-0787-8 (hc)
ISBN: 978-1-5127-0785-4 (e)

Library of Congress Control Number: 2015912956

Print information available on the last page.

WestBow Press rev. date: 09/29/2022

Our job in life is not to see through one another,
but just to see one another through.
—Dr. David J. Laurie

Dedication

This book is dedicated to our lovely daughter, Stephanie Ann Gilmour. Her brief four years with us were so precious! During that time, she asked Jesus into her heart and sang to everyone that she "got her ticket to heaven." Her sweet life was cut short by a traffic accident that changed our lives forever. This book was birthed out of her death, so we dedicate it to her and expect many people to experience a spiritual birth into God's family as a result. In such a way, we will see her death bring forth life.

Contents

Preface

Two very different worlds collided when I met my wife, Becky. She came from a small, rural family farm in southern Minnesota, and I came from the big-city life in both San Jose and LA, California. I guess God knew what He was doing when He placed us in the same class at Bible college in the fall of 1972 because I loved her as soon as I saw her. Still, I had a lot of work ahead of me to convince her to marry me and move away from the only life she knew—the family farm.

Our lifelong desire was to love the Lord our God with all our hearts, souls, and minds; to proclaim the truth of God's Word; and to help others find God's love. Though God's plans included some wonderful times, they also included some trials and difficulties that we couldn't have gotten through alone. This book was borne out of those trials and difficulties.

There were many phases the content of this book went through, but the death of our four-and-a-half-year-old daughter in a traffic accident was what truly welded Becky and me together and set us on a journey to write *Defining Life by Your Dreams Not Difficulties* as a way to help others through their own tragedies. In this book, we share what has been helpful to us in enduring and growing through our own pain. Some of the content was written and shared through a seminar we created called "Growing Through Crisis." After teaching it a few times, we modified it and renamed it "Navigating through the Storms of Life." Teaching the course at Celebration Church in Lakeville, Minnesota, afforded us the opportunity to enhance the information even more.

I had always intended to put the materials we had gathered into a book, but I was stuck. So, instead of a book, I took the stories we used in the seminar, and professionally recorded and produced them in a two-CD set called *Drive Time Inspiration*. The set is a compilation of twenty-one stories meant to encourage and help you push through difficulties. Even so, the idea of writing a book persisted.

More recently, Becky and I went on a family vacation to Kauai, Hawaii (which, by the way, I would highly recommend!). As I was sitting on the deck of the vacation condo, having a cup of coffee and praying for guidance in the lives of our family, I looked over the pristine golf course we faced and beyond it to the looming mountain drenched in waterfalls, and I thought about how blessed we were. As I enjoyed the view and the chirping birds flying around the deck, I envisioned the sun setting, the beauty disappearing, and the bird sounds fading away. I wondered at that moment, *If I cannot see or hear the beauty, is it still there?*

Some nights are long, and in places like Minnesota, there are long winters to accompany them. But since the creation of the world, morning has followed night, and spring has followed winter. Though the night is dark and quiet, the sun eventually rises, the birds return to singing, and green life comes back into view.

It was there all the time. It just needed some light.

Solomon said in Ecclesiastes 11:7, 8, "Truly the light is sweet, and a pleasant thing it is for the eyes to behold the sun. Yea, if a man live many years, let him rejoice in them all; but let him remember the days of darkness, for they shall be many." Solomon claimed there would be many dark days, but just remember what his father, David, said in Psalm 139:11, 12, "If I say, Surely the darkness shall fall on me, Even the night shall be light about me; Indeed, the darkness shall not hide from You, But the night shines as the day; The darkness and the light are both alike to You." The blessing of God is always with us; sometimes it's just out of view. We need to remember that God *is* light, and when we apply His truth to our lives, the light comes back. Don't allow the darkness to overtake you, but keep your focus on the light.

As I pondered this vision and my desire to write this book, I thought about the purpose of the book and tried to settle on a meaningful title. The summation of the book formed in my mind, *Defining Life by Your Dreams Not Difficulties.*

The title is symbolic of our vacation to Kauai, as the journey was a dream come true. Two years earlier, when the trip idea was birthed, we did not have the financial ability to go. But after forming a strategy, doing a bit of planning, and concentrating on saving—BAM! Two years later, we're standing on a sandy beach in Kauai, experiencing the ocean breezes and waves crashing at our feet. We were not only enjoying paradise, but also the lifelong dream I had of writing a book suddenly seemed doable.

So many of us look at why we *can't* instead of why we *can.* You may have faced difficulties and found disappointment. Your dreams may have taken a detour or gone out of sight completely. It is our prayer that this book will show you how to hope again— how to define your life by your *dreams,* not your *difficulties.*

—George and Becky Gilmour

Introduction

God did not leave us to our imaginations. Through His Word, He supplied us with principles and illustrations through people who both followed or disobeyed. If you are like me, you have spent a lot of your life wishing things would change and lamenting over things that haven't. We have all heard the regrettable epitaph, "Woulda, shoulda, coulda." I once asked a friend if he was happy. He paused for a moment and then said, "I was, just before you asked me that."

Have you ever wondered why the car's rearview mirror is so much smaller than the windshield? I believe it is because we are supposed to spend the bulk of our time looking ahead, not behind. The title of this book is a sharp comparison between the two mindsets with which we all live. One looks forward; the other looks behind. One holds hope; the other offers regret. One pursues promises; the other clutches problems. One brings us closer to solutions; the other leads us away from them.

David said in Psalm 27:13 and 14, "*I would have despaired* (given up hope); unless I had believed that I would see the goodness of the LORD in the land of the living. Wait for the LORD; Be strong and let your heart take courage; Yes, *wait for the LORD*" (NASB).

In other words, hope in the Lord, not in your circumstances. David believed God was the supplier of goodness, but he knew God doesn't always supply what we *think* is good, or work according to our timetable. David was anointed to be King of Israel when he was a teenager, but he was not able to take the throne until he was in his thirties. In the meantime, he spent most of those in-between years running for his life.

But David was confident in God's person and promises. He confirms that thought in Psalm 56:9. "When I cry out to You, Then my enemies will turn back; *this I know, because God is for me.*" What a statement—to know that God is for us! Well, if you know the Lord as your Savior, then you can say that too. But as we read in Psalm 27, it takes patience to see God's will unfold.

When we sit in the audience at the beginning of a play, we are privy only to what the opening scene reveals, but the stage director can see all the various activity going on behind the scenes. God is like that director. He not only knows what is going on behind the scenes, but He is also orchestrating them. David had learned to be confident in God's supply when his own resources ran out. Without that confidence in God's direction, he would have given up long before feeling the throne at his back.

All of us have unpleasant things attached to our pasts, but if we aren't careful, we can begin to live there. Many of us foster a slavery mentality by allowing ourselves to be chained to past difficulties and mistakes. We get stuck or stifled because our difficulties are more prominent in our minds than our dreams. No one benefits from the constant rehearsal of past difficulties. Doing so only promotes bitterness, confusion, and anger, and if you are tangled up in past issues, you won't have the creativity needed for future dreams.

God will not fix our past, but He does promise us a future hope (Jeremiah 29:11). He is calling us to look forward instead of behind; Philippians 3:13–14 says, "I have not achieved it, but I focus on this one thing: forgetting the past and looking forward to what lies ahead. I press on to reach the end of the race and receive the heavenly prize for which God, through Christ Jesus, is calling us."

When the chains of the past are broken, we are free to pursue our future and to look forward to what God has for us. It is our desire that the principles and stories revealed in this book will help you move from your past to your future and from your difficulties to your dreams.

CHAPTER 1

Shattered Dreams, Broken Hearts

When you pass through the waters, I will be with you; And through
the rivers, they shall not overflow you. When you walk through the
fire you shall not be burned, nor shall the flame scorch you.
—Isaiah 43:2

So why are we writing this book, and what has qualified us for the job? *A Tale of Two Cities* begins with the line, "It was the best of times. It was the worst of times." And there was never a time in my life when that line was truer than in the year of 1981. That year was a time of great experiences but also of shattered hearts. That year, Becky and I saw our flowering dreams crumble, and yet God brought us through it to be able to share the hope we can have in the living God, and to bring Him glory.

At the time of our tragedy, I was doing full-time ministry as an associate pastor and teacher at Anaheim Baptist Church and Academy. Becky was working full-time outside the home as an administrative assistant while also volunteering at church and taking care of the household. We had two beautiful children, a six-year-old boy named Jason and a four-year-old daughter named Stephanie. We were living our dream of working in the ministry and raising a family in Southern California.

But that year on a September evening, we experienced a parent's worst nightmare. While trying to cross a residential street, Stephanie slipped out of Becky's grasp and darted across the street. In a split second, a car hit Stephanie, and she was left motionless in the street.

The pain and agony of those next few minutes are impossible to describe. We were totally stunned, and our hearts felt as if they were being ripped from our chests. The ambulance quickly arrived and rushed Stephanie, along with Becky, to the hospital while I followed. We both felt as though we were suffocating and caught in a nightmare that would never end. We prayed as never before that God would spare our precious little girl. At the hospital, we waited in a private area for what seemed like hours but was probably only an hour when a doctor approached and we heard the words we had feared, "We're sorry, we did all we could, but we couldn't save her."

In that moment, all our dreams and hopes for her were shattered, and then the questions came. "Why did this happen to us, Lord? We've been faithfully serving You for years. Why Stephanie? Of all the unwanted children in the world, why her?" We hurt as if we had been kicked in the stomach. We were dealing with confusing emotions. We assumed that since we were walking with the Lord and working in the ministry, we should be protected from such a tragedy. The lie flitted through our minds, "If you had been 'better' Christians, this wouldn't have happened."

But the real truth we found through this situation was that we *are* protected and shielded from the effects of the storm, just not from all of it. The rain falls on the good and the bad, and the drought comes to the righteous and unrighteous.

Our families and friends gathered around. Some hugged us while others just sat with us in silence; it was all a comfort.

No words were necessary. People were showing they cared, and that was enough.

At Stephanie's funeral, several people dedicated their lives to God. Amidst our questions and pain, we saw their dedications for what they were—the first good to come from tragedy.

We knew Stephanie was safe in the arms of Jesus, but our lives were forever changed. Our son Jason was now too afraid to cross the street because he had witnessed his little sister hit by a car. The usual grocery list shortened. One more seat at the dinner table was empty. There were less chatter and giggling, and no more hair ribbons or dolls.

Our wounds were deep. For many weeks, we functioned on autopilot. In the book, *The Gift of Hope*, author Robert Veninga wrote, "Grief does carry its own anesthesia. It permits us to make decisions, to meet our responsibilities, and to carry on with our lives." We certainly found this to be true.

We held on to our faith in God and knew He was walking us through calamity. We met others who had lost a child, and they helped us see that we were not alone and that no one is exempt from pain.

We didn't blame each other, and we realized God was not to blame either. It was an accident. That was it. God was still good. We could have viewed Him as taking Stephanie away from us, but in truth, He had given her to us for four blessed years. We couldn't accuse him of being like Satan, who is the ultimate taker. Of course, God could have prevented it, and He didn't. But we believed in God's goodness, and therefore we knew that He must have wanted us to survive this and Stephanie not to, for good reason. He wanted to use our circumstances to draw us and others around us into a closer relationship with Him. Romans 8:28 states, "And we know that all things work together for good to those who love God, to those who are called according to His purpose." To be honest, we couldn't see the good at the time, but we claimed this verse by faith, and it became the catalyst for our lives and eventually for this book.

Slowly, we began to see Romans 8:28 grow into our lives but not without setbacks. Becky's Aunt Evelyn visited us for a month and helped Jason cross streets again. She was a blessing to our hearts as well, but still we dealt with triggers.

Our friend's little girl, who was near Stephanie's age, would wear Stephanie's hand-me-downs, and sometimes seeing her would fill us with grief all over again. One day, Becky happened to find Stephanie's favorite doll packed away, and she pulled out both the doll and the painful memories attached to it. We were hurting, but we could feel the prayers of our families and friends. We continued to cling to God's promise to never leave us or forsake us. One of our favorite comfort verses was Isaiah 43:2. "When you pass through the waters, I will be with you; And through the rivers, they shall not overflow you. When you walk through the fire, you shall not be burned, Nor shall the flame scorch you."

A while after Stephanie died, Becky had a dream. In the dream, Stephanie sat on her lap, hugged her one last time, and assured her she was okay and that everything would be all right. The dream was so real Becky could feel Stephanie's touch. Jason and I both experienced similar dreams as well. We believe God allowed us one last glimpse of Stephanie to help us heal and say good-bye.

Our daughter's death, the stress over issues at the church in Anaheim, and changes in our own spiritual direction caused us to reconsider our direction in life. We felt the Lord working in our hearts, pushing us toward a "new thing." So, at the urging of an old friend, we made the decision to leave Southern California and head to Austin, Texas, to check out a new church system with which he was involved. He even offered me a temporary roofing job.

Unfortunately, while working on a three-story apartment complex roof, I stepped too close to the edge, lost my balance, fell three stories through scaffolding and a walking plank, and landed on a pile of bricks. It was about that time I felt called to leave the roofing job for something a bit more grounded. Pun intended.

While recovering in the hospital, I awoke one morning to an audible voice saying, "George, you came here looking for a new container, but I am looking for new contents." The voice was so loud and clear it caused me to rise up in bed to see who said it, but there was no one.

All right, God, I thought. *I get it. We've been looking for a new ministry direction, but You want a new us.*

In the end, I had no broken bones or internal injuries, just a few stitches. Once again, we saw good come through pain, and we realized then that the accident was just a divine detour.

God is interested in building the image of His Son, Jesus, within us, but sometimes it takes something radical to get our attention. Though it might hurt at the moment, it is for our good in the end. It's up to us to let the director do His job.

By the end of 1981, we had experienced the following: the death of a child, relocation to another state, financial stress, new jobs, new friends, a new church, and a change in spiritual direction. By all the usual statistics, our marriage should have decayed, but our commitment to each other, and to the Lord, had only grown stronger.

Life was certainly different in Austin. We Midwesterners had never seen such large insects or felt such extreme heat for so many months out of the year. But we made good friends, and our broken hearts were already mending. We began to dream and plan again. We were even able to buy our first home.

But the calm didn't last. This time it took the form of an economic storm. During the 1980s, Texas was given to economic ups and downs, and at that particular moment, we were headed for a recession. The jobs and businesses we tried failed, and to top it off, our house devalued by $30,000, so we couldn't even sell it. We ended up walking away from our home and watching our only car get repossessed. We had barely gotten over the last tragedy, and already we found ourselves in another storm of lost possessions and deflated pride.

We wondered why God would allow this additional devastation when we'd already lost a child. But God was not done with us. He was still building our character and preparing us for His plan.

During the financial downturn, we felt the Lord leading us to a different church called Hope Chapel. This church became our spiritual hospital. We had been beaten up by our circumstances, and we were losing hope day by day, but at Hope Chapel, our hope was restored. There we learned that the Holy Spirit was not an "it," but a "He," and that He truly was our helper, as the Scriptures say.

We were mentored by home-group leaders and church pastors. We matured and felt as blessed to be there as we had upon first giving our lives to Christ. Our home-group leaders taught us that there were many blessing faucets: one of them financial, another one spiritual. Our financial faucet was off, but the spiritual faucet was on, so they encouraged us to stand under the spiritual faucet and immerse ourselves in God's blessings. And for three years, we did just that. During this time, we learned:

- God does care.
- God does have a plan.
- God did not abandon us.

- Time does not heal all wounds; sometimes they are sealed with scars.
- God is the great healer and provides the strength and direction for His plans.

But God did provide for us. We prayed for a vehicle, and God supplied a car. We prayed for money to pay rent, and God supplied it. Years later, we asked Jason if he remembered the hard times we went through in Austin, Texas. He said he didn't remember the hard times so much as he remembered us gathering as a family to pray for needs and seeing God provide.

We began to pray about God's purpose and dream for us. We also earnestly prayed for our dream—the ability to have another child. It was during our time at Hope Chapel that we really felt the Lord healing our broken hearts. I remember Becky and me praying one night for God to give us another child. A short time later, we discovered Becky was pregnant—a ray of hope during our storm.

Chad was born in 1987, and his birth gave us new hope. It was a dream fulfilled by our loving heavenly Father. Chad was a busy child, and he had a great sense of humor, even at a young age. He restored laughter in our house.

While our financial drought persisted, we continued to stand under God's spiritual faucet while praying for a solution. Even though we didn't realize it at the time, God had used Hope Chapel to help us learn how to define our lives by our dreams, not our difficulties. During this struggle, God strengthened us and gave us His promise in Jeremiah 29:11–14.

> For I know the plans (blueprints or dreams) that
> I have for you, declares the Lord, plans for wel-
> fare and not for calamity to give you a future

7

and a hope. Then you will call upon Me and Come and pray to Me and I will listen to you. And you will seek Me and find Me when you search for Me with all your heart. And I will be found by your declares the Lord and I will restore your fortunes and will gather you from all the nations and places where I have driven you declares the Lord, and I will bring you back to the place from where I sent you into exile.

We were contemplating moving back to Minnesota, where Becky's family lived. God heard the prayer of our heart and perfectly orchestrated the "how" for the move, and with the help of Becky's family, we returned to Minnesota.

God restored what we had lost.

- Family ties were restored.
- We had jobs again.
- We found joy in the Lord.
- He healed our broken hearts through prayer and the ministry of the Holy Spirit.
- He restored our self–esteem.
- He gave us the ability to minister to others.
- He gave us a house and some land.

But the greatest restoration of all happened within the last few years. God has given us two wonderful daughters-in-law, and so far, four precious granddaughters to love and spoil. God restored our ministry by placing us in another spiritual hospital called Celebration Church for several years, and this time we weren't the patients. God used us as lay pastors to minister to the fifty-five-plus PrimeTime Group, and more recently, we became Lifegroup pastors at River Valley Church. We continue to minister to people wherever God leads, but always we want to tell people that God is good, and His Word is true.

When looking at the two attitudes of defining life by either your dreams or your difficulties, ponder the following truths about both:

- One looks forward; the other looks back.
- One holds hope; the other holds regret.
- One contains promise; the other holds persistent problems.
- One brings solution; the other rehearses trouble.
- One brings life; the other brings death.

As devastating as the death of our daughter was, we refused to let our difficulties define our lives. God gave us new dreams, new relationships, and new ministry opportunities. Though we will always feel some of the pain, we have survived it with God's help and can now use it as an opportunity to help others. God has done this for us, and He will do it for you.

So will you choose to define your life by your dreams or by your difficulties?

> God is interested in building the image of His Son, Jesus, within us, but sometimes it takes something radical to get our attention, and it is for our good in the long run.

Thinking about It

1. What difficulties have you gone through? What do you do when you feel overwhelmed by negative circumstances?

2. What has God done in your life to fulfill the promise of Romans 8:28, "All things work together for good for those who are called according to his purpose"?

3. Do you know someone going through a difficult time that is similar to one of the situations you came through? How can you encourage them?

CHAPTER 2

Surviving Storms and Shipwrecks

But if we hope for what we do not see, we eagerly
wait for it with perseverance.
—Romans 8:25

It seems almost impossible to get through life without encountering storms and shipwrecks. You've probably already encountered your own version of a shipwreck, and it may have sounded like "Dear, this marriage is just not working; I want out. I've found someone else." Or maybe, "I'm afraid that the recent merger displaced your position. We have decided to reduce the number of managers and senior staff to achieve cost-cutting goals. You have been a good worker, and we will give you a good recommendation."

Shipwrecks come in many forms. Some of them may be the result of your decisions, while others might seem completely purposeless. In any case, we're often left with more questions than answers. *Why this? Why me? Why now? How am I going to get through this? Where is God in all this? What am I supposed to do?*

Scripture mentions the word "storm" thirteen times, but nowhere is there a more accurate picture of one than the scene mentioned in Acts 27. In this historical account, Paul is being transferred from Jerusalem to Rome to face what will be his doom, but they set sail during a stormy time of the year and face rough weather. Verses 1–13 indicated that the captain sailed against the odds, in the wrong season, and contrary to advice. In Acts 27:10–11, Paul counseled them. "Men, I perceive that this voyage will end with disaster and much loss, not only of the cargo and ship, but also our lives." Nevertheless, the centurion was more persuaded by the helmsman and the owner of the ship than by the things spoken by Paul.

This passage reads like a ship's log, even though Luke, Paul's attending physician, was writing it. Let's take a peek at it now and consider the events in this passage from the captain's perspective, as he might have written it in his journal.

Ship's log, AD 69

Entry #1: "We have encountered violent winds, and we were blown off course."

How about you? Have negative winds and circumstances blown you off course? Have you succumbed to the pressures, problems, or passions of your past? You may have been blindsided, or maybe poor decisions have gotten you mired. Sin always takes us farther than we wanted to go, steals more time than we wanted to give, and costs us more than we wanted to pay. But even so, new decisions can put you back on course.

Entry #2: "As a result of the adversity, we gave up and let the ship drift."

Have you ever felt so overwhelmed that you said, "I quit! What's the use?" The crew did, and Luke recorded that they felt like they were out there without a rudder. God's Word is our rudder if we choose to obey it. Second Peter 1:3 tells us God has given us *all* things that pertain to life and godliness.

Entry #3: "Although our journey is taking longer than normal, the winds have been somewhat manageable by sailing close to land. After transferring the prisoners and cargo to an Alexandrian vessel at Myra, we continued to sail. The winds picked up, and we were forced to sail very close to Crete. Paul of Tarsus, a prisoner I have somewhat befriended (and a follower of the infamous Jesus of Nazareth), concerns me greatly. His warning of impending disaster has stirred the crew. He does not recognize my need to get this cargo and this ship to Rome so I can get paid. I made a deal with him that I won't preach if he doesn't try to run my ship."

I find it interesting that almost all philosophies of life seem to work as long as everything is going well, but upon encountering opposition or adversity, only Jesus's resurrection remains truly powerful.

Entry #4: "Jerusalem, we have a problem. When the winds died down, I sailed on because the harbor we were at was not suitable for winter. I thought if we could reach Phoenix on the southwest side, we could dock there. Just when everything looked comfortable, we were hit by a northeaster. We've been blown off course. Due to the force of the gale, we could not steer the vessel. We had no choice but to let the wind drive us."

There are times when we are blown off course, and all we can do is wait to see what happens next. In these times, we must trust God because He is unchanging even when everything else becomes chaotic.

Entry #5: "We secured the skiff to the boat and ran cables around the ship to keep it together. There was a good chance we could be driven into sandbars, so we threw as much as we could overboard to lighten the load."

I am sure there have been times when you felt like things were out of your control, and you were forced to make difficult decisions. Tough times have a way of reprioritizing our lives and teaching us what really matters. It is always amazing to me how unimportant the things of this world become when our lives are in the crucible.

Entry #6: "The northeaster has not let up. We have been in this for almost two weeks, and the men are weak from sickness and strain. We have *no clear direction* since the storm clouds cover our heavenly navigation points. I can't see a thing! No sun, stars, or moon to navigate by."

It is easy in rough situations to lose both perspective and direction. Remember, this event took place before GPS or even compasses. How are you navigating through the issues of your life? A song I heard a few years ago said, "When you can't see His hand, trust His heart." The contrary winds of life can blow us in directions we would never have chosen to go. But we eventually discover that direction was exactly where God wanted us to go to fulfill His greater divine purpose for our lives and bring glory to His name.

Entry #7: "This may be my last entry, as *we have abandoned all hope.* The only shred of faith we have is coming from our resident nut job, who said, 'I told you we should not have sailed now, but be encouraged because I talked to an angel.' Wow. Now I've heard everything. Well, he says that we will all be saved because he has faith in God. Nothing else is working, so I hope he's right."

Abandoned—what an empty feeling! But that is where the

ship's crew and passengers ended up after trying everything they could think of to save the ship and stay afloat. Ever feel abandoned? Ever give up and quit? When nothing else is working, look to God and His church for the help you need to reset your sails and refocus on what matters.

Entry #8: "Well, we haven't died yet. We came close to an island Paul saw in a dream, so we ended up dropping four anchors after several depth tests and with concerns about striking rock. My concern now is that people might panic and jump overboard. If the storm doesn't kill me, the owner will when he sees what's happened to everything."

Interestingly, the crew dropped anchors to steady all four corners. When things become unsteady, we look for something to anchor us. When Becky and I lost our daughter, our *family* and *friends* were outstanding helpers. At times, our *fortune* (such as it was) brought us comfort by giving us the means to vacation and rest for a time. But the true anchor God gave us was *faith*. True *faith* is not anchored in temporary *fortune*, or mortal *family* and *friends*, but rather in the risen Christ, who was and is and is to come, and through whom and for whom all things were made.

Entry #9: "I don't know why I'm taking directions from a prisoner, but I feel a strange comfort and confidence in Paul. He has instructed no one to leave and claims that no one will be lost if we do what he says. Maybe his God is the right God. There were some loaves of bread left, and Paul had everyone eat some after he *thanked God* and blessed and broke it."

Many times it is easier to gain perspective when we sit, rest, get a little something to eat, and give thanks to the Lord. The storms we face are all a matter of perspective. From our points of view, the odds are often against surviving shipwreck, but the director, God, sees the scenes to come. Paul anchored his confidence in God and was able to give confidence to others because of it. He acted on his belief in God, not in the circumstances. Paul was able to keep his wits about him because he knew the Master of the storm.

The captain's final entry: "Paul had us cut the ropes to the four anchors that he emphatically told us to secure just a couple days ago. He said that no one would be hurt or lost, and it was time to just *trust God*. Well, he was right; everyone made it to shore, and the locals took care of us until we found another ship."

Even though valuable things were lost in this incident, everyone's lives remained intact, and God's power was made evident through it. Are you trusting God in the midst of your troubles?

In Matthew 8:24, we read about another storm. The Scripture says, "And suddenly a great tempest arose on the sea so that the boat was covered with the waves. But He was asleep." In Mark 4:35–41, the passage indicates that the disciples woke Jesus and said, "Don't you realize that there is a storm and we are going down?" Then Jesus arose and told the storm to quiet down, and the wind and sea became calm.

Many times in our crises, it seems like Jesus is asleep. We wonder, "Doesn't He know what we are facing here? How can He be so at peace when everything is coming apart?" It is at times like these the devil does his best work of helping us discredit God in our minds.

So where *is* Jesus when you need Him? I believe the Lord is always communicating with our spirits. The question is not whether He is broadcasting but whether we are listening.

Sometimes we just need to trust His Word. Jesus can bring peace in the middle of a storm. Don't be terrified by the winds of negativity, the clouds of terror, or the floods of turmoil. Just keep standing on the Rock of your salvation.

Fear of future circumstances can cause us to lose hope and become paralyzed. Don't allow fear to distract you from what God has given you to do. Instead, keep your eyes fixed on Him and His cause.

Matthew 14:22–33 tells of another storm. In this setting, Jesus asked his disciples to travel across a lake so He could be by Himself for a while. Surprise! Another storm brews up.

Jesus, seeing the disciples' peril, walks across the stormy water. Upon seeing Him, they are frightened because they think Him a ghost.

Sometimes Jesus comes to us in the middle of a crisis, and we don't recognize Him because we are so consumed by the problem that we don't see the solution. But Jesus comes to His disciples and simply says, "Don't be afraid, it is I." Jesus was up on the mountain, interceding for them, watching to make sure they were okay, and He is doing the same thing for us today. Do you think that in the middle of your crisis, Jesus is interceding for you as well?

In Mathew 14, Peter recognized Him and said, "If it's really you, just say the word, and I'll come to you." Jesus told Peter to come, and Peter took off and started walking on the water with Jesus. But as he saw the waves and began to sink, he cried out, "Lord save me!" and immediately Jesus reached out and grabbed him. Many criticize Peter for having a lack of faith, but no one else stepped outside the boat.

How about you? Will you sit in a boat with complacency and criticism, or will you step out faithfully into what God is calling you to do, no matter how impossible it looks?

To get through your storms, you need to stand on solid ground. In Matthew 7:24–27, we have the story of the wise man who built his house on a foundation of rock, while the foolish man built his house on a foundation of sand. When the windstorms, rain, and floods assaulted the houses, only the one on the solid rock foundation endured.

When Becky and I went through devastating storms, the Lord encouraged us to not cower in the corner of our house, listening to the howling winds and driving rain. Instead, He told us to stand strong on our foundation, Jesus Christ, the solid Rock, and rely on His strength and protection to get us through.

In these passages, we can see that Jesus was more in control while sleeping than we are while awake. He is the Master of the storm. In the middle of it all, God uses difficult situations to draw us to Him. The intensity or longevity of the storm will determine how close we get to the Lord and how strong our faith becomes. Often the things we are going through prepare us for what lies ahead and enable us to help others going through similar situations.

Remember—Jesus is always watching and looking out for us.

Tough times have a way of re-prioritizing our lives and teaching us what really matters. It is amazing how unimportant the things of this world become when our lives are in the crucible.

Think about It

1. What kinds of storms have you come through or are you currently going through?

2. Study Matthew 7:24–27 and determine which kind of foundation your life is built on.

3. How can you keep from abandoning all hope?

CHAPTER 3

The Impossible Dreams Become Possible

And we know that all things work together for good to those who
love God, to those who are called according to His purpose."
—Romans 8:28

In this chapter, we have two stories of slaves living nearly
four thousand years apart. They were both victims of their
circumstances, and they both had dreams that, when fulfilled,
changed their respective nations.

Sometimes the dreams we have seem to be completely impossible. However, it does not mean you should stop dreaming
or praying! Booker T. Washington, known only in his younger
years as Booker, had a dream to get an education, but at the time
that dream was illegal because slaves were not allowed to go to
school. But in January 1863, the Emancipation Proclamation
changed everything.

Booker's family moved off the plantation and traveled to
West Virginia. Booker took jobs in both a salt mine and a coal
mine, but the work was hard and dangerous. While in the coal
mines, he heard about Hampton Institute, a school for blacks.
To Booker, Hampton Institute sounded like heaven, and he
resolved to go, though he didn't know how he would get there.

He then heard about a job opening in the household of General Ruffner, the owner of the coal mine. He applied and he was hired. Mrs. Ruffner was a Yankee known to be a strict taskmaster, but Booker reasoned that it must be better than working in the coal mine.

He soon learned that she wanted everything cleaned in a systematic and prompt manner. He performed the work to her specifications and eventually won her trust. Mrs. Ruffner allowed him to attend school for an hour a day during winter months. She saw his potential and encouraged him to pursue his dream of an education.

Booker saved almost $100, which would cover his entrance into the Hampton Institute. As he was just about to leave for school, his stepfather told him that he had lost his job and the family was in serious jeopardy. So Booker gave the family most of the money he had earned, and he was left with only a few dollars. Still, he felt compelled to go, so at age sixteen, he walked nearly five hundred miles to Virginia and prayed that God would supply him with funding.

Talk about relentless.

Booker knew that even poor students could get an education at Hampton Institute through paying their way by working. However, the head teacher, a Yankee woman, was suspicious of his country ways and ragged clothing. He told his story to the teacher, including his dream to learn and willingness to do whatever it took. At the end of the day, Booker approached the teacher again. And she told him the adjoining recitation room needed cleaning. After she had left, Booker was outraged that she had given him no hope, yet expected him to clean one of the rooms. But as he thought about it, he realized that she had just given him his first test.

The next day the teacher thoroughly inspected the room,

using her handkerchief to check for dust. Upon finishing, she decided the room had been cleaned to her satisfaction, and she promptly enrolled him in the school. She hired Booker as a janitor, which allowed him to work to pay for his education. Booker stated that one of the most valuable things he received at Hampton Institute was the understanding of the use and value of the Bible.

In one respect, Booker had come full circle, back to earning his living through menial labor. But his entrance to Hampton eventually led him away from a life of forced labor for good by giving him the chance to become an instructor. He was quite the orator, and he was asked to speak on a circuit for several thousand dollars a year. But he turned it down because his dream was bigger—to start a school for students just like him.

He started a night school named Tuskegee Institute, so those working during the daytime could still get an education. All of these experiences prepared him for his destiny. He was hired as the principal and guiding force behind Tuskegee, which opened in 1881. Through his work at Tuskegee, he became recognized as the nation's foremost black educator. The concept of self-reliance borne of hard work was the cornerstone of Booker's social philosophy.

A man who overcame near-impossible odds, Booker T. Washington is best remembered for helping black Americans rise up out of the economic slavery that suppressed them long after they were legally free. The Emancipation Proclamation freed the black slaves *from* slavery, but in most cases, they were not freed *to* be equal to their white counterparts. Booker worked hard to change this, but it took another hundred years and the Civil Rights Act of 1964 to free black Americans to equal treatment and opportunities.

The legacy of Booker's life and focus was the Tuskegee

Institute that educated black Americans. The Tuskegee Institute birthed the Tuskegee Airmen, who played a significant role in World War II. Booker's fight helped them find the courage to fight two wars, one within and the other without. Another legacy of Booker's was a young man named Jackie Robinson, whose courage set a pace for those who would follow him. It is said that Booker's autobiography, *Up from Slavery*, gave Jackie the courage to be the first professional black baseball player.

What are you willing to do in order to accomplish your dreams? Most who accomplish great things must overcome great obstacles to do so. Maybe all you need to get where you want to go is some good old-fashioned Yankee grit, and even though you won't like how it comes, accept it as a gift from God, getting you ready for your main assignment in life.

The God who makes the impossible possible does not just hand us blessings. Instead, blessings come as the result of our obedience and pursuit of Him. Look at the history lesson that Moses gave to his people in Deuteronomy. He reminds them that the exodus was a struggle and that the dream of a promised land had come at a price.

Interestingly enough, the Israelites had to fight for their inheritance. I have always thought it odd to have to fight for one's inheritance since an inheritance should be automatic. I guess you might say that the inhabitants of the land were contesting the "will." The Israelites had been given a great opportunity, but they would have to fight for it.

Over three thousand years after Deuteronomy, it seems that the Israelites (Jews) are still fighting for their inheritance, but the victories have given them the fortitude to continue fighting. God is committed to His plans and dreams for us, even when we lose sight of them.

As we read the Bible and see those who struggled through

their circumstances and overcame all obstacles, we are blessed and given the courage to continue on the path God has laid out for us. Look once again at Deuteronomy 28:2, and you will see that God not only blessed the Israelites for their obedience but that the *blessing overtook them.* The blessings of God are pursuing us and are set to overtake us if we only obey the voice of God.

Let's take a look at another slave named Joseph, who was an Old Testament patriarch. Imagine, one day all of your siblings ganged up on you because they were jealous of the relationship you had with one of your parents. Maybe you don't have to imagine. In Joseph's case, the brothers' jealousy brought them to the point of plotting to kill him.

But one of Joseph's brothers prevailed, and instead of killing Joseph, they sold him to a group of gypsies headed to Egypt. They killed a lamb, smeared its blood on Joseph's famous coat of many colors (a gift from their father and a source of their anger), and gave the coat to their father along with the lie that a lion had caught and killed his beloved son Joseph.

Meanwhile, the gypsies sold Joseph as a slave in Egypt, and he became the servant of an important officer in the Egyptian government. Although absent from his father and in alien territory, Joseph performed well in his position. The officer he worked for had a wife who evidently was less than impeccable. Joseph was a good-looking young man, and she tried enticing him into her bedroom. Joseph resisted to the point of escaping from her and leaving his robe that she had grabbed in her hands. Upset and feeling slighted over her advances, she told her husband that Joseph tried to rape her and that in fighting him off she had managed to grab his robe.

Well, so much for Joseph's position in that household. He was immediately taken to jail and left to die. But I believe the officer knew his wife and her lustful ways, and he ordered Joseph to prison to save face. Had he really believed or known that Joseph was guilty, he probably would have had Joseph executed instead of imprisoned.

So there Joseph sat, in prison, knowing that he had done nothing to deserve the treatment he had received from his brothers or the treatment he had received from the officer who owned him. Joseph found himself on a detour, and one could hardly blame him if, at that moment, he doubted God's provision.

Genesis 39:21 says, "But the LORD was with Joseph, and showed him mercy, and gave him favor in the sight of the keeper of the prison." This seems to imply that Joseph had it easy, but Psalm 105:18 claims Joseph was bruised on his feet with chains and had to wear an iron collar.

Though he was protected from death by the favor of God, the experience was less than excellent. I've wondered why he had to go through such an ordeal while being such a faithful servant of God. But verse 17 of Psalm 105 says that God sent Joseph to Egypt just prior to a great famine and intentionally arranged for him to be sold as a slave. The purpose of the difficult experiences Joseph had is revealed in verse 19, which states that God allowed Joseph's character to be refined through difficulty until the time came to fulfill God's promises to him.

As I prayed over this passage for understanding, I felt the Lord tell me that this process had to take place because if Joseph had been elevated directly from the officer's household to second in command in Egypt, it would have infected him with pride. The prison experience gave him a great discomfort and distaste for Egypt and taught him that this place was not his place, these people were not his, and their gods were not his God. That is why when Joseph later had children, he named them with Hebrew names—Manasseh—"causing to forget" and Ephraim—"I shall be doubly fruitful."

During this time in prison, Joseph advised a few prisoners who were being released, but they forgot about him until the pharaoh had a dream that he couldn't understand. The former prisoner told the pharaoh about Joseph and his ability to interpret dreams, and Joseph was summoned from the prison.

Joseph not only interpreted the dream about a coming seven-year period of prosperity followed by a seven-year period of famine, but also shared God's plan to survive the seven-year famine. As a result, the pharaoh placed him second in command in order to execute the plan. That plan ended up being so successful that word spread back to Israel that Egypt had enough grain to help them in the same famine.

That is how Joseph's former family from nearly thirty years ago came back to him. Joseph's father, Jacob, sent his sons to Egypt, minus Benjamin, the other "favorite son." The boys were to negotiate a purchase of grain to sustain them for the remainder of the drought. Not going into a lot of details, as you can read it for yourself in the latter half of Genesis, Joseph recognized his brothers during the grain transaction, but they did not recognize him. Eventually, Joseph revealed his identity and the brothers feared for their lives, thinking that Joseph would have them killed for what they had done to him. But Joseph trusted God through his circumstances and knew there was a bigger purpose at play. He said to his brothers, "But as for you, you meant evil against me; but God meant it for good, in order to bring it about as it is this day, to save many people alive" (Gen. 50:20). Joseph's dream and destiny had been fulfilled, and it only took forty years.

What is the moral of the story? Joseph's faith in God sustained him through the times of rejection, abandonment, slavery, and imprisonment. He knew he was righteous, and so his conscience was clear.

How has your attitude been through your trials? How has your attitude been in times when you've been treated unjustly?

Whatever you are going through, you may be assured that God is there, and *He has not* forsaken you. What you are going through may just be what is necessary to accomplish His will *through* you, and as a result, God, not you, will be glorified. Joseph's continued faith and loyalty to God in the face of adversity not only sustained him, but also allowed God to use him to save the nation of Israel, through which the Messiah would eventually be born.

The point of Joseph's trials was that in order to be trusted, he had to be tested.

So how is your test coming? You know, if you don't pass, you get to take it over. Remember, God is not overwhelmed by your circumstances, and there might even be a good chance that He is allowing them to make you into what you really want to be. Your faith and confidence in God through these times may also lead to a great victory.

If Booker's stepfather had not needed Booker's tuition money, Booker would not have needed to get a job at Hampton Institute, and the connection may not have been made for him to become a great teacher and orator through the administrator of the school.

Now remember what Joseph said to his brothers. "What you meant for evil, God meant for good." Often God turns the circumstances we consider bad into something good. Even tragedies.

We thought that leaving Austin, Texas, in the late eighties was a terrible thing because we had been maturing in our faith at Hope Chapel. But in the end, God moved us back to family, where we have blessed each other and been given jobs where we have flourished. Our sons received great educations, established their careers, and found their spouses, and we found our purpose—helping people define their lives by their dreams, not their difficulties.

Let the stories of these two dreamers bolster your confidence in the knowledge that God knows what He is doing and has your best interest at heart.

God knows what He is doing and has your best interest at heart.

Think about It

1. What is "Yankee grit" and how do you get it?

2. Have you experienced an injustice? How did you handle it?

3. Reflect on an incident where God turned something "bad" into something "good." Share this story with someone this week.

CHAPTER 4

What You Overcome May Define Who You Become

These things I have spoken to you, that in Me you may have peace. In the world you will have tribulation; but be of good cheer, I have overcome the world.
—John 16:33

L ife can be brutally difficult. Robert Schuller, the famous pastor of *Hour of Power*, wrote a book titled *Tough Times Never Last, But Tough People Do!* I heard evangelist Lowell Lundstrom say many times, "I felt like I attended the University of Adversity where the school colors are black and blue, and the school cry is 'Ugh!'" I must admit, I too felt like both a student and graduate of that school. How about you?

When you look back at difficult times, you have the luxury of looking back with, hopefully, more wisdom and a better perspective. Some of those experiences might still be fresh, while others might seem like they happened a hundred years ago. When you are in the center of a calamity, everything seems to be in slow motion. You feel like nothing is ever going to end. You wonder, "What is the purpose of this pain?"

Paul talks about the race of life in 1 Corinthians 9:24–27, as he uses images from sporting events he must have witnessed. I believe that if Paul were still alive today, he would be a fan of the Olympics (and maybe even football!).

> Don't you realize that in a race everyone runs, but only one person gets the prize? So run in such a way to win! All athletes are disciplined in their training. They do it to win a prize that will fade away, but we do it for an eternal prize. So I run with purpose in every step. I am not just shadowboxing. I discipline my body like an athlete, training it to do what it should. Otherwise, I fear that after preaching to others I myself might be disqualified. (NLT)

God wants us to run the race of life and not waste time. All of us can give excuses and reasons why we can't overcome circumstances. When you are faced with seemingly insurmountable situations, remember: in the struggle to overcome the tragedy, you will find your destiny.

In a tragic, rural country-school fire in the early 1900s, a young boy was badly burned, and his brother was killed. At the hospital, the doctor informed the boy's mother that the boy's best chance of survival was to amputate the most burned leg. She responded by telling the doctor that she had just buried one of her sons and did not intend on taking only half of her other son home. She asked for instruction on how to treat her son's legs and then took him home.

The mother began a daily regimen of physical and spiritual therapy that usually brought both of them to tears, as she massaged his taut, burned limbs. She refused to believe the doctor's *prognosis* but rather believed God's *promise* found in Isa. 40:31:

"But those who wait on the LORD Shall renew their strength; They shall mount up with wings like eagles, they shall run and not be weary, They shall walk and not faint."

The spiritual therapy from God's Word gave them both hope. She kept repeating, "They shall run and not be weary, walk and not faint. They shall run and not be weary, walk and not faint." One therapy repaired his body, and the other, his spirit. Over time, the therapy worked, and to the doctor's amazement, the boy went from walking to running. Overcoming our handicaps is often what gives us the strength and determination to become what we were meant to be.

Now, if you had been alive in the 1930s, you would have known the name of this young boy who was told he would never walk again—*Glenn Cunningham*. Well, contrary to his diagnosis, Glenn eventually ran into the history books by setting world records in the mile and receiving a silver medal at the 1936 Olympics.

Colonel Sanders struggled to overcome the failure of his business due to a road construction project in front of his restaurant. This caused him to look for a buyer for his famous fried-chicken recipe. He spent over a year on the road, even sleeping in his car at times, until he finally found a buyer, and KFC was born. Seven years later at the age of 75, Colonel Sanders sold his fried-chicken company for a "finger-lickin'-good" $2 million. When other people would have quit and filed bankruptcy while lamenting their bad luck, Col. Sanders persisted with his dream.

Henry Ford failed and went broke five times before he finally succeeded at developing the assembly line. As a result, he is credited with single-handedly creating the middle class of America. He coined the phrase, "Whether you think you can or think you can't –you're right!"

Walt Disney was fired by a newspaper editor for; "lack of ideas." Walt also faced financial difficulties before he built the amazingly successful Disney empire. Disney stated, "All the adversity I've had in my life, all my troubles and obstacles, have strengthened me… You may not realize it when it happens, but a kick in the teeth may be the best thing in the world for you."

In 1954, the manager of the Grand Ole Opry fired *Elvis Presley* after one performance. He told Presley, "You ain't goin' nowhere, son. You ought to go back to drivin' a truck." Elvis Presley went on to become the most popular rock-and-roll singer in America.

Dave Dravecky, pitcher for the San Francisco Giants in the late eighties, lost his arm to cancer. Imagine going from pitching for a team headed to the World Series to not even having an arm within a couple months' time. That difficulty could have consumed his life, but instead, he allowed God's love and grace to redirect his destiny. Having found a relationship with Christ while in the minor leagues, he also discovered that God could turn tragedy into a blessing. Dave and his wife created their Endurance Ministry, specifically to encourage those who are facing serious illness, loss, or depression. We benefited from their encouragement when we spoke to a ministry representative who stated, "Dave will never get over missing his arm, but he will get through it. And you will never get over the loss of your daughter, nor should you have to, but you will get through it."

Just a few years before winning the Super Bowl, *Kurt Warner* was working the graveyard shift stocking shelves at a local supermarket so he could train to be an NFL quarterback one day. He got an opportunity to play arena ball and, consequently, was seen by a scout, which brought him to the NFL. Kurt never stopped pursuing his dream to play professional football.

Chuck Colson went from a prestigious position in the White House to prison, to faith in Christ, and then to found a ministry. Chuck Colson was special counsel to President Richard Nixon from 1969 to 1973 and became infamous during the Watergate scandal. He pled guilty to obstruction of justice and consequently served seven months in the federal Maxwell Prison in Alabama. Imagine the humiliation.

But God had a plan for Chuck. During that humbling experience, he found Christ his Savior, and his life changed radically. As a result of his prison time and conversion, he founded Prison Fellowship, which works behind prison bars, reaching men and women with the Gospel. He also spent the latter part of his life focused on Christian worldview teaching and training. He was a public speaker and author of more than thirty books, and he was awarded the Templeton Prize for Progress in Religion for his exceptional contribution to affirming life's spiritual dimension. Chuck was able to overcome his past humiliation and embarrassment to be greatly used by God to transform lives so that prisons release disciples of Jesus Christ—not repeat offenders.

Wilma Rudolph was born prematurely, the twentieth of twenty-two children, and doctors did not expect her to survive. As a young child, she contracted pneumonia, scarlet fever, and polio, which damaged her left leg. Doctors said she would never walk again without assistance, but her mother told her she would. She believed her mother, and at age nine after her mother's special care, she took off the metal brace and was able to run and play like other children. At age eleven, she started playing basketball and became quite athletic. During college, through the direction of her coach, she became a member of the track team at Tennessee State University. In 1960, Wilma broke an Olympic two-hundred-meter dash record and became the first American woman to win three gold medals at a single

Olympics. That same year, the Associated Press named her US Female Athlete of the year. What would have happened if she had given up?

Here's an additional story to ponder when you think that what you are going through is just too difficult. In 2001, a unique story hit the airwaves of our local music scene. It was about a very gifted, internationally known Minnesota guitarist named *Billy McLaughlin,* who was diagnosed with a neuromuscular disorder called focal dystonia. The disorder caused uncontrollable movement in his fingering hand, resulting in unintended notes being played. It appeared that his twenty-year music career had come to a conclusion. However, in 2006 he reemerged onto the music scene having overcome the effects of the disorder. No, it wasn't cured; something even more incredible had happened—he relearned how to play guitar left-handed because the disorder didn't seem to affect his natural picking hand.

Those of you who play guitar know what a challenge it would be to learn to play with the opposite hand. This feat was absolutely amazing, and he is still as entertaining today as ever, even though today the symptoms are as bad as before. Billy did not succumb to the disorder, but with "outside the box" thinking, he proved that you can overcome.

I find it interesting that in the concluding chapters of the Bible, the theme of overcoming is presented by the Lord Himself. In the opening chapters of the book of Revelation, several churches in the area were encouraged to overcome their fear, depravity, poverty, persecution, and other concerns. In each of the seven cases presented, there was an admonition as well as a reward. In my recent reading of that book, I realized that God would not have challenged us to overcome if it were not possible. With His help, anything is possible.

So what do all of the people discussed in this chapter have

in common? They did not allow the tragedies or difficulties of life to define them. They did not let their lives become a series of excuses or complaints. The bottom line is that none of our difficulties can keep us from God's will. What matters is that you overcome the difficulties with God's help and never give up on the dreams He's given you.

> Overcoming our handicaps is often what gives us the strength and determination to become what we were meant to be.

Think about It

1. Reflect on what difficult situation you have overcome or are currently trying to overcome?

2. What parts do determination and persistence play in overcoming your difficulty?

3. What part does God's divine intervention play in your being an overcomer? Have you asked for His help?

CHAPTER 5

Moving Mountains and Getting through Valleys

Multitudes, multitudes in the valley of decision!
For the day of the LORD is near in the valley of decision.
—Joel 3:14

Theodore Roosevelt, twenty-sixth president of the United States, once said, "In any moment of decision, the best thing you can do is the right thing, the next best thing is the wrong thing, and the worst thing you can do is nothing." Everyone has been in the valley of decision. Maybe you're still there. Perhaps you have choices in front of you, but fear freezes you. You have made poor decisions before, and now you are worried you'll make more.

Many of you have not ended up where you intended. Your "perfect" financial decision did not work out. The person you thought was a friend stabbed you in the back. The person you thought you married became someone else.

On the other hand, there may have been times when it became necessary to modify your plans. For instance, while in college, my pastor friend with whom I had previously worked invited me to come out to his church in Anaheim, California, to assist him. I anticipated being able to come right on staff when I arrived, but that was not the case. They weren't capable of providing me a salary, and instead, I discovered he really needed me more for friendship, ideas, and stability. It took four years of working in another profession while laboring in the church as a lay pastor before the door to full-time ministry finally opened.

We actually ended up creating enough ministries within the church that the need arose for a full-time administrative position I could assume. However, I was starting to enjoy what I was doing in my other job, so when the time came to choose one way or the other, I had to think carefully. My wife and I prayed about it, sought counsel from trusted friends, and analyzed what we really felt called to do. As a result, I became the full-time assistant pastor at Anaheim Baptist Church for the next four years.

Looking back on when we first got to Southern California, we were very confused about whether we had been listening to God or ourselves. I had packed up all our earthly belongings into an eight-by-five trailer and moved my pregnant wife and myself across the country on faith. But once there, reality didn't meet our expectations. What to do, what to do? I have to confess, my attitude was less than excellent, and I wondered why God was allowing this to happen. Had I made the wrong decision?

Then one evening I came across a ministry program on TV that I had never seen before. The program was Dwayne Friend and his Gospel Guitar. That day he taught from a passage in 1 Kings 20 about Syria's King Ben-Hadad, who was intending to wage war against Israel's King Ahab. Ben-Hadad told his men to tell Ahab he was coming and that he intended to take all Ahab's gold, silver, wives, and children. After hearing the threat, Ahab said, "Do what you will."

But Ben-Hadad was looking for more of a fight than that, so he sent his servants back with more detail of his intentions. That worked! King Ahab gathered the elders of the city together, explained the situation, and received advice and direction.

A prophet of God told Ahab that God would secure the battle in Israel's favor. There is a lot more detail given in the passage, but the bottom line is that Ahab won and Ben-Hadad decided to back off for a while and return the next year. Ben-Hadad's reasoning was that his army had been defeated in the hills because Israel's God is a god of the hills, but Ben-Hadad's god was a god of the valley. First Kings 20:28 says, "Then a man of God came and spoke to the king of Israel, and said, Thus says the LORD: Because the Syrians have said, The LORD is God of the hills, but He is not God of the valleys, therefore I will deliver all this great multitude into your hand, and you shall know that I am the LORD."

God is both God of the mountains and God of the valleys. He is God when the bank account is full and God when it is empty. He is God when we are healthy, and He is God when we are ill. He is God when everything is going great and God when everything is going wrong. This was the revelation that we needed and would revisit again, more than once.

As I mentioned, the opportunity for which I was looking was on hold, but my finances were not. The other job that I pursued did not work out. I had to provide for my soon-to-be family, and I hit a snag. Now what do I do?

Well, I tried sitting around and sulking for a while. That didn't help at all. So after hearing Pastor Dwayne's message on TV, I prayed, asked for forgiveness, and moved forward.

Sometimes we experience paralysis from overanalyzing situations. Why this all happened was not as important as "What should I do next?" I was honest, willing to work hard, and dependable. Those were my credentials, and that was what I used to get the next job. However, I never took my eye off the goal of full-time ministry while on a temporary detour.

It is easy to get stuck in our circumstances. Sometimes

we think we didn't hear God correctly or that we have done something wrong. But remember, David said in Psalm 23:4, "Yea, though *I walk through* the valley of the shadow of death, I will fear no evil; For You are with me; Your rod and Your staff, they comfort me." David found himself in many valleys in his lifetime. He wasn't excited about living in, wandering in, or camping in the valleys. But he was walking *through* them.

How are you handling your challenges? Sometimes we don't get through our situations overnight. Think about the poor woman mentioned in Luke 18:1–8.

> Then He spoke a parable to them, that men always ought to pray and not lose heart, saying: 'There was in a certain city a judge who did not fear God nor regard man. Now there was a widow in that city; and she came to him, saying, 'Get justice for me from my adversary.' And he would not for a while; but afterward he said within himself, 'Though I do not fear God nor regard man, yet because this widow troubles me I will avenge her, lest by her continual coming she weary me.'" Then the Lord said, "Hear what the unjust judge said. And shall God not avenge His own elect who cry out day and night to Him, though He bears long with them? I tell you that He will avenge them speedily. Nevertheless, when the Son of Man comes, will He really find faith on the earth?"

I was always confused about the last verse because it seemed disconnected from the rest of the story. However, as I was reading it again a couple years ago, the Lord showed me that the whole point of the story is wrapped up in the last sentence. Faith is persistent. She knew what she needed, and she was not going to give up until she got it. She kept knocking. When Jesus taught the disciples how to pray, He told them to keep *asking*, keep *seeking* and keep *knocking*. Interestingly enough, the first letter of each of those commands spells *ASK*!

Sometimes there are mountains in our lives that need to be moved. Mountains of debt, mountains of grief, mountains of pain, and mountains of fear will overshadow us throughout our lives. So how do we get to the point where they don't dominate our lives? Jesus explained in Mark 11:22–25. "So Jesus answered and said to them, 'Have faith in God. For assuredly, I say to you, whoever says to this mountain, "Be removed and be cast into the sea," and does not doubt in his heart, but believes that those things he says will be done, he will have whatever he says. Therefore I say to you, whatever things you ask when you pray, believe that you receive them, and you will have them. And whenever you stand praying, if you have anything against anyone, forgive him, that your Father in heaven may also forgive you your trespasses.'"

There are some keys in this passage. First, God tells us to speak to the mountain, not just think or pray about it. That same instruction is given for salvation in Romans 10:9–10, 13 where Paul said "that if you confess with your mouth the Lord Jesus and believe in your heart that God has raised Him from the dead, you will be saved. For with the heart, one believes unto righteousness, and with the mouth confession is made unto salvation. For whoever calls on the name of the LORD shall be saved."

It is necessary to inform your head and declare to the heavens, your intentions. The word spoken by you needs to be spoken in confidence, knowing the truth of God's Word. When we pray for mountains to be moved, we are to pray not only believing that we are praying for His will to be done, but also thank Him that it has already been done. Lastly, remember that we are to have a clear and clean conscience toward God and all others. Grudges and bitter resentment in our hearts can and will get in the way of our prayers.

Before I learned some of these lessons, and when so many things went wrong (according to our plans), I remember hearing Andraé Crouch's song, "Through It All." The last verse, especially, spoke to my heart and situation because the words reminded me that it is through difficulties that we learn to trust God. Then the more He solves problems, the more we trust Him and can thank Him for the difficulties.

The darkest valley I ever experienced was the tragic loss of our daughter. I remember the feeling of complete helplessness as I ran to her lifeless body lying on the street. As I failed to resuscitate her and then as the ambulance drove to the hospital, I wondered, "Why is this happening to Stephanie? What did I do to deserve this?"

As an associate pastor, I had been at the bedside of many who were at the end of their lives, but the words of comfort I spoke in those situations just stuck in my throat. I prayed all the way to the hospital for God to take me instead of her. But He didn't.

I called Becky's folks and then my own, and I heard them cry on the phone. I remember, at the funeral, laying my head on my dad's shoulder and saying, "This really hurts."

"I know," he replied.

Years before, when I was just three months old, he had come home early from his naval assignment because my mom was very ill. Nine days later, she died in an iron lung, a victim of lung polio, a mere thirty-four days after their first anniversary. Suddenly the twenty-five-year-old seaman had the emotional consequences of the death of his wife and a three-month-old son to care for while enlisted in the Navy. Yeah. He knew it hurt. He felt it himself.

I remember being so busy around the days leading up to my daughter's funeral, with so many people to meet, and calls and arrangements to make. But the graveside was overwhelming. As they lowered the casket in the ground, I realized more than ever that there would be no more kisses, cute dresses, proms, or any of the expected activity of watching your daughter grow up. It all ended right then and there.

Afterward, I remember crying at the drop of a hat and feeling guilty for the times I didn't cry. But though our house might have been messed up, God had a bigger plan, and as Psalm 23 promised, He walked with us through that valley, gave us great comfort, and taught us His truths.

God did not abandon us. God will not abandon you. He is committed to your maturity. So when you think about the situation in which you feel stuck and you wonder how you are going to get out of it, remember this passage in Isaiah 49:15 that says, "Can a woman forget her nursing child, and not have compassion on the son of her womb? Surely they may forget, yet I will not forget you. See I have inscribed you on the palms of My hands."

God knows who you are and where you are, and He knows what is going on in your life. Your circumstances do not take God by surprise. Whether it is a valley to get through or a mountain to climb or move, the decisions you make must be based on the truth of God's word. God loves you. He will get you *through* the valleys and *over* the mountains. Go to Him with the impossible.

God will not abandon you! He will get you through it!

Think about It

1. What situation have you faced where you felt abandoned? Who came to your rescue?

2. Why is it important to speak your intentions or declare what you want out loud?

3. Reflect on a journey you took through a valley and journal how God walked through the valley with you.

CHAPTER 6

Knocked Down But Not Out!

I have fought the good fight, I have finished the race, I have kept the faith.
—2 Timothy 4:7

The Olympics were in vogue during Paul's lifetime, and he tended to use athletic illustrations in his writings. You may have heard of our modern-day Ultimate Fighting Championship (UFC). One such Olympic event in Paul's day was probably more akin to the UFC than to traditional boxing, and it's not hard to imagine Paul using it as an illustration in 2 Corinthians 4:8–10, 16–18, when he wrote, "We are pressed on every side by troubles, but we are not crushed. We are perplexed, but we are not driven to despair. We are hunted down, but never abandoned by God. *We get knocked down, but we are not destroyed.* Through suffering, our bodies continue to share in the death of Jesus so that the life of Jesus may also be seen in our bodies. That is why we never give up. Though our bodies are dying, our spirits are being renewed every day. For our present troubles are quite small and won't last very long. Yet they produce for us a glory that vastly outweighs them and will last forever! So we don't look at the troubles we can see right now; rather, we fix our gaze on things that cannot be seen. For the things we see now will soon be gone, but the things we cannot see will last forever" (NLT).

The following more-modern boxing story illustrates the message of this passage.

The year is 1952, and the auditorium is packed and buzzing with anticipation because the audience knows the fight tonight will go down as the greatest fight any of them will ever see. The young upstart Rocky Marciano, also called the "Brooklyn Bomber," has earned his chance to take on the World Heavyweight Champion, "Jersey" Joe Walcott, who ascended to the top with his dazzlingly quick footwork and lightning-fast hands. *Ring* magazine once did a frame-by-frame comparison of Walcott's jab against Muhammad Ali's jab at similar stages of their careers, and found that Jersey Joe Walcott threw four jabs in the time Ali threw three. And they weren't weak jabs, either.

Yes, Rocky Marciano seemed to have an uphill battle ahead of him. Word spread through the underworld that Marciano would not be allowed to take the title unless he knocked Walcott out. Walking to the ring, Marciano was even told by a detective, whom his manager had hired to look into the rumors, that he couldn't win by a decision but that he would have to knock Walcott out completely in order to win the fight.

Imagine that you have earned the right to be in Marciano's position, and not only are people betting against you, but also they're even willing to cheat to ensure the odds are in the other person's favor. That's rough.

As the fight begins, cheers come from everywhere. It seems the battle has been going for merely seconds, and then it happens. Marciano goes down after Walcott lands the same blow that he used to knock out two previous opponents. Walcott turns to the crowd with raised hands, believing the fight is over, but as he turns around to watch the referee count

Marciano out, he's amazed to find Marciano standing again and ready to go.

Two rounds go by, and an eye problem begins taking its toll on Marciano. For four rounds, Marciano is virtually blind, and both sides blame each other for using the curative substance called "dynamite" on the cut by Marciano's eye, which is known to cause blindness. Nevertheless, as a result, Marciano is taking a beating.

In the thirteenth round, Walcott steps to the ropes and shifts in order to sucker Marciano into range. It works and he throws a right, but at the same time, Marciano throws his own and snaps Jersey Joe Walcott's head around, immediately slumping the champ to the floor.

The referee begins counting as the crowd gasps. "Eight, nine, ten, *out!*" The referee rolls Jersey Joe Walcott on his back, and he's still unconscious. Some whisper, "Is he dead?" Others wonder if he'll ever walk again.

The December 1952 issue of the *Ring* reported, "While Charley Daggert kept counting over the fallen champion, there was never a twitch from Walcott as he lay crumpled on the canvas. The spectators looked on in awe. Many feared that old Jersey Joe had been fatally injured, so tense was his body."

All the referees favored Jersey Joe Walcott at the time of the knockout, confirming that Rocky Marciano, in fact, won the fight only because he knocked Walcott out.

Maybe some have counted you out. Maybe you have counted yourself out. Life can be a tough fight, and at times, it may feel easy to succumb to the odds. But you must keep fighting on.

Now dial forward about fifty years to take a look at the fictitious boxer, Rocky Balboa. In the sixth and final installment of the Rocky series, Stallone portrays his character in a comeback opportunity that bothers his son, who is tired of living under his dad's shadow. After his son is finished complaining about his own life, Rocky gives him some advice. I can't help but believe Stallone is interjecting his own philosophy in this scene.

"You, me, or nobody is gonna hit as hard as life. But it ain't about how hard you hit, it's about how hard you can get hit and keep moving forward. How much you can take and keep moving forward. That's how winning is done!"

Wow, what a message! I think that is exactly what Paul was writing about in 2 Corinthians 4. I can just hear God saying, "Get up and keep moving forward!" God has great promises and plans for us, but they don't come without a struggle. What we have to keep in mind is that the battle is the Lord's, and He already owns the victory. What we are going through is a journey of faith, a journey toward trusting God and his promises. Second Chronicles 20:15 and 17 explains: "Thus says the Lord to you; Do not be afraid nor dismayed because of this great multitude for the battle is not yours, but God's. You will not need to fight in this battle. Position yourselves, stand still and see the salvation of the Lord, who is with you, O Judah and Jerusalem! Do not fear or be dismayed; tomorrow go out against them, for the Lord is with you." Proverbs 21:31 states, "The horse is prepared for the day of battle, but deliverance is of the Lord."

Like in the Rocky movie, we are challenged to take what life throws at us, and then rise again and run after our destinies. Just because it is your dream, or God's dream for you, don't think you won't have to fight to get it.

If you have been knocked down, get up and pursue your dream. Go get 'em champ!

God has great promises and plans for us, but sometimes they don't come without a struggle. What we have to keep in mind is that the battle is the Lord's and He already owns the victory.

Don't Quit

When things go wrong, as they sometimes will,
When the road you're trudging seems all uphill,
When the funds are low and the debts are high,
And you want to smile, but you have to sigh,
When care is pressing you down a bit
Rest if you must, but don't you quit.

Life is queer with its twists and its turns,
As everyone of us sometimes learns,
And many a failure turns about
When they might have won, had they stuck it out.
Don't give up though the pace seems slow,
You may succeed with another blow.

Often the goal is nearer than,
It seems to a faint and faltering man,
Often the struggler has given up
When he might have captured the victor's cup;
And he learned too late when the night came down,
How close he was to the golden crown.

Success is failure turned inside out
The silver tint of the clouds of doubt
And you never can tell how close you are,
It may be near when it seems so far;
So stick to the fight when you're hardest hit,
It's when things seem worst that you must not quit!

—Author unknown

Think about It

1. Why is it important to keep getting up when you get knocked down? Who is there to help pull you up?

2. How do you react when you hit a brick wall? What can you do to get through your obstacles?

3. What dream are you fighting for right now?

CHAPTER 7

Finding Treasure in Your Trash

Redeeming the time, because the days are evil.
—Ephesians 5:16

Imagine finding a million-dollar item in the trash. Well, Charles E. Terrill didn't have to imagine it, because he found a painting worth about $1 million in the trash of a Senate office building in Washington, DC, while working as a congressional representative's aide in the early eighties.

Fourteenth Street at Sixth Avenue was painted by John Sloan during the Great Depression in 1934, and the painting hadn't been seen by the public since 1939. It was painted on the back of an old board instead of canvas, and it ended up in the garbage because its value was unrecognized by the person who placed it there.

Another story: one Connecticut pipe-cleaning company was hired to clean an underground sewer pipe, and in the midst of the usual gunk found in the sewer pipe, workers discovered sixty-one rings, vintage coins, and silverware pieces. Although the workers had a very unpleasant job, something good came of it—they were allowed to keep the treasure they found (Maxwell, *Winning with People*).

While teaching our seminar, "Navigating through the Storms of Life," Becky and I met a married couple who had experienced a devastating fire in their mobile home. The family escaped unharmed, but their personal possessions, clothes, and mementoes were destroyed. About a year later, on the wife's birthday, her mother-in-law, with whom she did not have a close relationship, gave her a large gift box to open. The wife opened the box, found it full of potpourri, and thought the gift odd, but as she sorted through the potpourri, she felt a book. When she pulled it out, she discovered it was their wedding album. Her mother-in-law had combed through the charred remains of the fire wreckage the day after the tragedy and found the wedding album, amazingly spared from any serious damage. She took it home, kept it in potpourri to get the smoke smell out, and then gave it to the wife for her birthday. The wife's attitude and relationship with her mother-in-law was instantly changed. Through this tragedy, she found the real treasure from the trash—a renewed relationship with her mother-in-law.

Imagine finding treasure in your own trash. You may have experienced some setbacks or detours, but something good came out of those detours. You may have contact names on the back of unwanted pieces of paper or important phone numbers on the side of a McDonald's hamburger bag that is now in the trash. Maybe your attitude is in the trash because someone else decided to spread their bad day around and you inadvertently allowed them to spread it on you. Yes, you may have some very valuable ART (*A*ttitude, *R*ecords, *T*ime) in your trash.

When I look at professional sports teams, it seems the aspect that most differentiates teams is their *A*ttitudes. In baseball, many teams battle through their whole season just for a chance to get into the playoffs. It's a bonus if they happen to get a bye on their first game or get home-field advantage for the first game. But the Yankees assume those are givens. They feel they had a bad year if they are not in the World Series, let alone winning it. Unfortunately, our attitude is too often in the trash because, as Zig Ziglar said in *See You at the Top*, we become SNIOPS—Subject to the Negative Input of Other People. Don't let other people's attitudes dictate yours. Choose to stay positive.

Well-known pastor, teacher, and radio celebrity, Charles Swindoll, wrote the following many years ago.

Attitudes

The longer I live, the more I realize the importance
of choosing the right attitude in life.
Attitude is more important than facts.
It is more important than your past;
more important than you education
or your financial situation;
more important than your circumstances,
your successes, or your failures;
more important than what other people think or say or do.
It is more important than appearance,
your giftedness, or your skills.
It will make or break a company. It will
cause a church to soar or sink.
It will make the difference between a
happy home or a miserable home.
You have a choice each day regarding
the attitude you will embrace.
Life is like a violin.
You can focus on the broken strings that dangle,
or you can play your life's melody on the one that remains.

You cannot change the years that have passed,
nor can you change the daily tick of the clock.
You cannot change the pace of your march toward your death.
You cannot change the decisions or reactions of other people.
And you certainly cannot change the inevitable.
Those are strings that dangle!
What you can do is play on the one string
that remains – your attitude.
I am convinced that life is 10% of what happens to me
and 90% how I react to it.
The same is true for you.

Such timely words! We all have disappointments and heart-aches, and they're through no choice of our own. Science has determined that no individual is able to process both positive and negative information simultaneously. We do not have the capacity to innovatively and creatively devise solutions for future needs while we are caught up with current or previous problems (Tracy, *Maximum Achievement*). Unfortunately, most people's minds are tied up with negative possibilities and the fear of potential disasters. We must stop focusing on and rehearsing our problems. Instead, we must focus on the promises of God, and on pursuing our dreams and keeping a positive attitude.

Rumor has it that a little boy wanted to be the greatest hitter in history, so he took his baseball and bat into his backyard. He threw the ball up, let it drop, and swung inaccurately. He tried over and over and over but could not hit the ball. He decided he would try one final time. He strategized, calculated, threw the ball up, let it drop, and swung as hard as he could and... missed again. He ran into the house with seeming amazement, and announced to his family that he had instead become the greatest pitcher in history.

It's a matter of perspective and attitude. When attitudes outdistance abilities, even the impossible is possible (Maxwell, *Your Road Map for Success*).

Did you know Post-it Notes were the result of a failed glue experiment?

Many years ago, a man trying to invent a new tension spring for the navy found he had instead invented the Slinky when it accidentally fell on the ground.

Penicillin was created accidentally by a frustrated scientist who was trying to invent a cure-all drug. In disgust at his failed attempts, he threw the petri dishes away. He later noticed that the mold in one of the dishes was eating all the bacteria away.

Potato chips were invented in a fit of rage as a restaurant customer kept asking for his potatoes to be cut thinner and fried longer. The cook, in anger, sliced the potatoes so thin you could read the newspaper through them, and fried them as hard as a rock. Evidently, the customer loved them and wanted more, and so did others.

While trying to invent a rubber material that would not deteriorate upon exposure to jet fuel, a 3M scientist dropped some of the compound on her shoe and instead invented Scotchgard.

We could go on and on talking about seeming failures and the great good that came out of them, but the message is the same: it all comes down to one's perspective and attitude.

How's your *Attitude*? Does it need adjusting? Then listen to people who are where you want to be, and see what you can copy. Why reinvent the wheel? Listen to or read positive motivational materials. Ask your mentors what has made them so successful and how they have managed to keep going in such an economy. You're never too old to learn.

Now what about your *Records*? Records and journals are gold! They keep getting more valuable, but it does take work to create and maintain them. As a matter of fact, this book is the result of an accumulation of journal entries and other writings over many years. I encourage you to record your victories, and the words God has given you so that you can reflect on His blessings.

Tom Peters, in his book, *In Search of Excellence,* said that the top one hundred companies in America are the top one hundred not because of their talent in the technical, but because of their brilliance in the basics. Keeping records of your visits and conversations is basic to your success, but keeping accurate and easily retrievable records is as hard as digging for gold. The outcome speaks for itself whether for business purposes or to leave a personal family legacy. I, for many years, lived on scraps of paper and even smaller pieces of memory. That leads to being underfunded every time! Value your files so you can prepare before meetings and sound intelligent when calling a client back. Remind them of the things that you discovered that were important to them. They will appreciate your efficiency and be more apt to have confidence in you for future commitments, services, or products. Whether you prefer electronic devices or old-fashioned paper planners, it doesn't matter—just consistently and systematically keep records.

So what about your *Time*? James 4:14 says, "Whereas you do not know what will happen tomorrow. For what is your life? It is even a vapor that appears for a little time and then vanishes away." Time is something we all have in common. Whether you're a prince or a pauper, you only get twenty-four hours a day. What you have done with it will determine what kind of a return you will get on your investment. If you made $100,000 a year and you worked forty hours per week, your time would be worth nearly $50 per hour. Think about that the next time you are tempted to waste your time on something that has little or no value.

My former boss used to say that in the office-equipment business, there is a ninety-day cycle. If you are living in poverty today, you were probably doing something other than planting the seeds of success ninety days ago. The reality is that if you are doing the same thing now, you will be getting the same harvest ninety days from now. The contacts you make today are like seeds. Use your time wisely and plant seeds you would like to harvest. Then the harvest will come.

If you pursue life with the right attitude and take good notes along the way, you will have a legacy for others to follow and a record of great memories along the way. Learn from your mistakes. Learn from others' mistakes. Be with people who encourage you and pull you up instead of down. Make sure you cultivate your *Attitude*, *Records*, and *Time* like precious ART.

In the movie *Saving Private Ryan*, the last words of the lieutenant played by Tom Hanks to Private Ryan were, "*Earn this!*" In other words, do something with your life that made all the sacrifices worthwhile. Make sure, when it's all been said and done, that your life counted for Christ.

I have a four-and-a-half-year-old daughter in a graveyard in Anaheim, California, for whom time ran out early, and I have a picture of her with one of my aunts who passed away years later at age ninety-eight. None of us knows when our time is up—use it wisely and keep looking for the treasure in your trash.

> We must stop focusing on and rehearsing our problems. Instead, we must focus on the promises of God and pursuing our dreams.

Think about It

1. Are you looking for treasure in your trash, or are you making trash out of your treasure? What treasure have you found recently?

2. Why is attitude so important?

3. Do you realize that God treasures you? Deuteronomy 14:2

CHAPTER 8

Overcoming You

If anyone desires to come after me, let him deny himself
and take up his cross daily and follow me.
—Luke 9:23

H ave you ever met people who just can't get over themselves?
They are always talking about their achievements, problems, and needs. The world is basically all about them, their
opinions, and their perspectives. I used to know someone just
like that—me! It continues to be a challenge. Have you noticed
that when we are in a group and have our picture taken, we
want to see ourselves more than anyone or anything else?

Ella Wheeler Wilcox wrote a poem about two kinds of people, lifters and leaners. Lifters are pleasant people who add
something to life. They desire to help others by "lifting" their
load and intentionally make life more enjoyable. Leaners, on
the other hand, steal value from others and think only of themselves, taking people down in the process. Instead of lifting
their shares of the load, leaners make the load heavier by re-
lying on lifters. If you don't know how to be a lifter, then you
are probably a leaner by default. Do you make people feel like

blessings? Or do you make them feel that they always come up short (Canfield, Hansen, & Hewitt; *The Power of Focus*)?

It is difficult to train ourselves to be become interested in others, and to ask them questions and discover interesting things about them without having to match or "one-up" them. But why is this trait so hard to change?

Well, humanity tends to be selfish. In Deuteronomy 6:5, Moses summed up the Ten Commandments in this way: "You shall love the LORD your God with all your heart, with all your soul, and with all your strength." Jesus restated this in Mark 12:29–31. "Jesus answered him, The first of all the commandments is: 'Hear, O Israel, the LORD our God, the LORD is one. And you shall love the LORD your God with all your heart, with all your soul, with all your mind, and with all your strength.' This is the first commandment. And the second, like it, is this: 'You shall love your neighbor as yourself.' There is no other commandment greater than these." The reason Jesus said the greatest of all the commandments was to love God with all we have and to love others as ourselves is because this is harder to do than to keep all of the Ten Commandments.

So what is my point?

The point is, much like a problematic computer, our lives have a built-in virus. A virus, as you may know, is an infectious parasite that destroys information and disables programs in our computer. Well, the virus in our lives, known as sin, is similarly destructive. Sin, by acronym, is stubborn, independent nature. It makes us rebel against authority, do evil, and avoid good.

For instance, on paper we may know that gambling is a dumb way to try to make money. However, our emotions and greed get the best of us when we are put in front of a machine or card table, and we continually throw good money after bad. The more we lose, the more we try to get it back. A little win, once in a while, just baits us to continue until we are broke. I've often heard it said that the best way to come out of a casino with a small fortune is to go in there with a large one.

So why do we do stupid things when we know what is right? Good question. The following fictional story may help us understand this phenomenon better.

A man named John was a ranch hand on a large ranch in Oklahoma. A friend of the owner of the ranch came over one day and noticed John chopping wood out by the barn. Every time John swung the ax, he said, "Oh, Adam, oh, Adam!" The friend inquired about John's peculiar behavior. The owner explained that John learned in church that when Adam sinned, God told him that he would have to work six days by the sweat of his brow. The owner said, "Ever since then, John has been unhappy with Adam and blames him for the hard work he must do." The friend then told him about an idea he had, and the owner decided to employ it.

The ranch owner's friend rode off, and the owner proceeded to tell John that he was going to town to do some business and would be gone until Saturday. He told John to do the chores that needed to be done and that he could enjoy all the comforts of the ranch. He could even stay in the main house, if he so desired. But there was only one stipulation. The owner had put a cake tin on the kitchen table and told John to leave it there and not move it. Soon after, the owner left and John continued with his chores.

By the second day, John became increasingly curious as to why the cake tin could not be moved. His curiosity became so great that by Friday he could not even stay in the house. On Saturday, John thought that since the owner would be home soon, moving the tin would have little effect. He proceeded to enter the house and pick up the cake tin. To his surprise, a small mouse that had been eating some cheese scurried away. John tried and failed to catch it.

When the ranch owner arrived home—you guessed it!—he immediately went to the kitchen and discovered the empty cake tin. Turning to John, he said, "You know I gave you the whole ranch and only asked you to leave this one thing alone. But just like Adam, you could not resist."

The owner's friend came over on Monday afternoon and noticed John out by the barn chopping wood again, only this time, every time he chopped he said, "Oh, John! Oh, John!"

You see if we were Adam, we would have made the same choice he did. And when Adam failed, humanity was infected with the sin virus. After Adam chose to eat the fruit with his wife, he became aware of his *self*, and he ran and hid. When God confronted him, Adam blame-shifted, made excuses, and tried to fix the problem himself. This was the first precedent for humanity set in the Garden of Eden. Adam became rebellious, independent, and selfish, resulting in eviction from his perfect environment.

After many thousands of years, it appears the human race has not changed much. Humanity could not handle the knowledge of good and evil without making the wrong choice. God was the only one who could handle that choice successfully, and so He devised a more permanent solution to Adam and Eve's cover-up than fig leaves—a lambskin made into clothing. Unfortunately, the only way for that to take place was for the lamb to be killed. What was innocent died for those who were guilty.

Pastor David Laurie, originally from Glasgow, Scotland, was the pastor of the church in Sunnyvale, California, where I began attending when I was in high school. Pastor Laurie told a story of going to his uncle's sheep ranch in northern Scotland one spring while in his early teens. After looking through the herds and noticing all the new baby lambs, he came across a problem. One of the ewes had died giving birth, leaving a lamb with no mother. Another lamb had fallen upside down into one of the wagon wheel ruts and suffocated as a result of the lungs pushing down on its small heart.

To young David, there was a simple solution. Simply place the orphaned lamb next to the ewe who had lost her lamb, and it could nurse from her. The only problem was that when he tried this plan, she butted it away. David then tried again, but he was met with the same response. His uncle explained that it would never work. Why? Because the mother could smell which lamb was hers and would only nurse her own. To David's surprise, his uncle then took the dead lamb, skinned it, put its hide over the orphaned lamb, and pinned it underneath.

David thought this was harsh, until he realized his uncle had created the perfect solution—an acceptable substitute. The ewe allowed the orphan lamb to nurse because the baby now smelled like her own lamb. The one lamb's death gave life to the other lamb. This is exactly what God did for us in allowing His Son, Jesus, to taste life and death as a man. Jesus's innocent blood was shed so it could be applied to our sins—He died and rose again that we might have eternal life. It is applied by faith when we admit our sins before the Holy Father and accept His solution. John 3:16: "For God so loved the world that He gave His only begotten Son, that whoever believes in Him should not perish but have everlasting life."

The Apostle Paul paints a pretty dim view of humanity in Romans 3:10–18. He says that no one is righteous, not even one. He also says that no one is wise or truly seeking God and that humanity has turned to his or her own ways and is not interested in doing what is truly good. The next few verses simply declare that we *all* are really messed up. Verse 23 then states that we have *all* sinned and fallen short of God's requirements for going to heaven.

"So now what?" you may ask.

Well, the truth is, if we do not accept God's remedy, then we are on our own when we die. Hell is a place made for Satan; however, we will join him there if we reject God's gift of salvation.

But there is another option! Paul says in Romans 5:8, "But God showed His great love for us by sending Christ to die for us while we were still sinners" (NLT). So now, where does that leave you? Romans 10:9, 10, and 13; "If you confess with your mouth that Jesus is Lord and believe in your heart that God raised Him from the dead, you will be saved for it is by believing in your heart that you are made right with God, and it is by confessing with your mouth that you are saved… For everyone who calls upon the name of the Lord will be saved" (NLT).

The solution for our sin virus is pretty simple—accept the gift of salvation through the shed blood of Jesus, the Lamb of God. If you have never accepted Jesus's shed blood as payment for your sin, do it now, just pray this prayer out loud:

Jesus, You died upon a cross
And rose again to save the lost
Forgive me now of all my sin
Come be my Savior, Lord, and Friend
Change my life and make it new
Help me, Lord, to live for You.

—"The Salvation Poem" by Matt & Sherry McPherson

If you just prayed that prayer and meant it with all your heart, your sin virus is removed and you have a new start with

God as your heavenly Father. The Lord now sees you as His own and is walking beside you to guide you in fulfilling your God-given purpose in this life and give you an eternal home in heaven.

These things I have written to you who believe in the name of the Son of God, that you may know that you have eternal life.

1 John 5:13

Think about It

1. Who do you like being around, the lifter or the leaner? Which one are you?

2. Has your sin virus been removed by accepting God's gift of salvation through Jesus shed blood?

3. Do you know for sure you will spend eternity in heaven with Jesus when you die?

We would love to help you get started in your new abundant life with Jesus, so please contact us for information on the next step as a follower of Jesus!

Contact us at: defininglife2@gmail.com
Visit www.thesalvationpoem.com

CHAPTER 9
The H Factor—HOPE

Why are you cast down, O my soul? And why are you disquieted within me?
Hope in God, for I shall yet praise Him For the help of His countenance.
—Psalm 42:5

Hope deferred makes the heart sick, But when the
desire (dream) comes, it is a tree of life (joy).
—Proverbs 13:12

I would have lost heart **(hope) unless I had believed** that I
would see the goodness of the Lord in the land of the living.
—Psalm 27:13

I was trying to land on one of the three verses above to begin this chapter, but all three seemed to work together toward the same message. Most of us use the word "hope" to say, "I hope so." But these three verses are but a few that tell us not just of the *possibility* of hope, but also of the *power* of hope. They tell us about hope, encourage us to have hope, and explain what happens when hope is either delayed or fulfilled. But to really understand hope, we need a good definition of what it is. We also need the reason why hope is necessary. We need to understand how to use it and, more importantly, how to have hope when everything looks hopeless.

Interestingly enough, hope is mentioned seventeen times in the book of Job, while the much longer book of Psalms only mentions it twenty-five times. When you look at the context of Job, you would think it is much more about things that are hopeless.

So what exactly is hope? I examined the word in its various uses from both the Old and New Testaments. I looked at the word in Hebrew, Greek, and English and came up with this homogenous definition: Hope is *the joyful anticipation of expected outcome.*

The "joyful" part came from the Greek translation as it related to the attitude one would have from expected good news. The "expected outcome" contradicts the more casually stated phrase "I sure hope so." In the end, the etymology of the word is much more positive than "I sure hope so" would have us believe.

There is no greater illustration of hope than that of Jesus himself. Almost every action He took flew in the face of the social values of the day. To the Romans, who were in political control, He was a threat because He claimed to be the King of the soul, and as such solicited worship. To the Pharisees, He was a threat because the key value of His Kingdom was love, not rules. He upset the social standards when He said that he who is least is the most in God's Kingdom, and if you would be greatest, you must be the servant of all. To the common person, Jesus was his or her hope because Jesus was not indifferent to their circumstances. He said in Matthew 11:28–30, "Come to me all you who labor and are heavy laden and I will give you rest. Take My yoke upon you and learn from Me, for I am gentle and lowly in heart, and you will find rest for your souls, For My yoke is easy and My burden is light." For the poor, their burdens were heavy with many religious and political tasks. However, Jesus's ministry foretold in Isaiah 61 that He was coming to give good news to the poor, healing to the broken hearted, and freedom to the captives. That was a proclamation of hope!

So how do you get hope when everything looks hopeless? *First of all, look to God, not yourself.* Only God can deliver real hope because real hope can only come from something transcendent, meaning something more powerful and from outside our world. Psalm 146:5 says, "Happy is he who has the God of Jacob for his help, whose *hope* is in the LORD his God."

A number of years ago, a friend shared her story of surviving a devastating divorce. She thought her marriage was going fine, and she enjoyed being a stay-at-home mom taking care of her home and family. That all changed one night when she was handed what felt like a live hand grenade—divorce papers. She was distraught and had no idea what to do.

Everything in her life was coming apart, but she had children whom she loved and who needed her. She realized she needed to get a job to take care of herself and the kids. She looked to the Lord for help and options. She thought about becoming a teacher because she loved teaching children in Sunday school at her church, but since she did not do well in school, she had concerns about going to college. She decided to trust God and move forward, so she enrolled in college and secured babysitting for her kids. She was acting on the truth found in Philippians 4:19 that says God will provide for our needs and in Jeremiah 29:11 that says God has a plan. She believed that God would help her, that He had a plan for her success, and that He was helping her build a future and a hope. She successfully completed college, secured a teaching position, and she has been an outstanding teacher for many years. Our friend's life was no longer defined by the tragedy of divorce; she pursued

God's dream for her, and God made a way for her where there seemed to be no way! Isaiah 43:19 says, "For I am about to do something new. See, I have already begun! Do you not see it? I will make a pathway through the wilderness. I will create rivers in the dry wasteland." If God can do this for her, He can surely provide the resources and assistance you need in your circumstances.

Secondly, believe in the word of God instead of your circumstances. Psalm 130:5 says, "I wait for the LORD, my soul waits, and in His word I do *hope.*" According to Hebrews 11:1, "Now faith is the substance of things hoped for, the evidence of things not seen." Faith has a substance (foundational reality) and is the substance of things hoped for (that which allows us to wait for its accomplishment), and therefore, faith is based in hope. Faith also has evidence (proof or conviction) in things not seen in this reality.

Hebrews 11 contains a long list of people from the Bible who exemplified hope. They defied their circumstances, trusted God, and stepped out in faith. The passage starts out with Abraham, who obeyed God's voice, left his home and family, and went to an unknown location with the hope of receiving the inheritance God promised to give. The passage then ends with those who were martyred for their belief in Jesus's saving power, and the hope of the resurrection.

We can have confidence in the truth of God's Word, even when the circumstances defy logic, because our confidence and hope are not in the things of this world but in the God who created the world.

Thirdly, believe that the current situation is not the end. Hebrews 10:23 says, "Let us hold fast the confession of our hope without wavering for He who promised is faithful." We are to trust God and His Word even though the circumstances look difficult because God is always faithful and loving.

Circumstances often betray God's reality. The tendency is to create our beliefs based on the circumstances instead of defining the circumstances by what we believe God's Word says. What a daily battle!

One day, while eating in a restaurant with a friend, we got into a conversation with our server and found out she was a single mom with two young children to support. We sensed she could use some divine intervention in her life, so we talked to her about the love of Jesus and invited her to our Sunday church services. She started coming regularly and did indeed accept Jesus as her Savior. Over the next couple years, our families developed a friendship. One day she came to me and wanted my advice. She told me that she was now twenty-eight years old and was thinking of going back to school to become a lawyer in the hope of better supporting herself and her children. But law school would take four years, and she would be thirty-two years old when she finished. She wondered if it was too late for such a plan. I asked her, "How old will you be in four years if you don't go to law school?" She replied, "Thirty-two." I said, "It sounds inevitable! The real question then is, do you want to be a thirty-two-year-old lawyer or a thirty-two-year-old server?"

She came to the realization that her difficult situation was not the end and that she had options to change her situation. She believed God's word, Philippians 4:13: "I can do all things through Christ who strengthens me," and Philippians 4:19: "My God shall supply all your need," and Deuteronomy 31:8: "And the Lord, He is the One who goes before you. He will not leave you nor forsake you; do not fear nor be dismayed." She put action to her dream and indeed became an attorney. Was it hard and uncomfortable at times? You bet it was, but the pain of change and moving out in faith was less than the pain of staying stuck in her circumstances.

Lastly, praise and hope in the Lord even though you don't feel like it. David said in Psalm 71:14, "But I will *hope* continually, and will praise You yet more and more." Worship is our spiritual weapon against the enemy of our soul battling against us to steal our faith and joy. When we praise God and sing to the Lord in our times of despair or chaos, we are acting on our hope and walking by faith to the victory God has already won.

Darlene Zschech, the famous Christian songwriter and worship leader from Australia, told of a time when her family faced great financial need without any foreseeable way of tackling it. One day, while overwhelmed by the situation, she went to her music room, poured out her heart to the Lord, and wrote and sang a song to comfort her soul. She had initially written it for herself and her family's benefit and did not think it would have value as a worship song. However, after a fellow worship leader heard it, he encouraged her to give it to the world. That song, called "Shout to the Lord," became her signature song in 1993 and was published in 1996. It has been calculated that approximately 25–30 million people per Sunday are singing the song worldwide. The song ministers to people every day, especially the phrase, "Nothing compares to the promise I have in You." The promises of God are where we can find true hope.

When we are convinced of the dream God has given us, we are able to patiently wait for its accomplishment. Take a look at Elijah in 1 Kings 18:43–45. At the end of a three-year drought, God promised to send rain, Elijah told his servant to eat and drink for he heard the sound of abundant rain even though it was not evident in the natural. He told the servant to go up and look toward the sea for evidence, and it took seven times before there was any visible signs. Even then, it was just a cloud the size of a man's hand. Elijah told the servant that the cloud was proof and to get going before the rain overwhelmed him.

It's interesting that Elijah heard the rain before the earthly evidence was there. Elijah was listening to God instead of the natural. Nearly nine hundred years later, Jesus would teach his disciples to pray, "Thy kingdom come, Thy will be done on earth as it is in heaven." Sometimes God gives us insight into the realm of His Kingdom, and our senses respond to that. What is God telling you to do, and what is He showing you in your dreams?

While working as an assistant pastor at Anaheim Baptist Church, I felt God tell me to put up a tent on our church playground to lead an old-fashioned tent-revival meeting. The senior pastor and deacon board felt it would be too much of a production for a congregation the size of ours, and a big financial risk.

The following Sunday the Lord used a message from a visiting speaker to move me to continue pursuing what I felt God was leading me to do. I put a lot more thought and detail into the presentation the second time to the senior pastor and the deacon board. Finally, the senior pastor and deacons saw the benefits and jumped on the idea. The new plan included using the tent for vacation Bible school (VBS) in the morning with a major Bible character coming out of a time machine each day to teach the lesson to the kids, and then having special music and preaching in the evening. I delegated all the specifics of the VBS to very qualified people and helped organize the evening service. The event was advertised in the local newspaper, and we handed out flyers and invited people from the neighborhood. The event was a smashing success with many people coming to the tent meeting and making a decision to follow the Lord. It became a pivotal point in the church's growth. Later, I found out that sixty years prior to our event, an evangelist by the name of Gipsy Smith had held an old-fashioned tent revival in the very same area.

The tent experience taught me to always make sure the Lord's voice is the loudest voice I'm listening to. As we pray, we must seek God's face and read His word. We might hear Him speak to our heart or show us things to come. "My sheep hear my voice…and they follow me," Jesus said in John 10:27. However, if our confidence is in the world, we will miss His voice and insight. We must place our confidence (hope) in Him, trust His word, and then step out in faith when the time comes.

It is often more common for people to shrink back in fear than to step out in courage. If that is happening to you, use the formula Pastor Londa Lundstrom Ramsey shared in a Sunday morning message, "When I don't know what to do, I keep my eyes on You." The message came from 2 Chronicles 20 where the fear of the circumstances drove the king to prayer, not paralysis. "'Do not be afraid nor dismayed because of this great multitude, for the battle is not yours, but God's" (verse 15). "And when he had consulted with the people, he appointed those who should sing to the LORD, and who should *praise the beauty of holiness*, as they went out before the army and were saying: "Praise the LORD, For His mercy endures forever" (verse 21).

We can praise the Lord even before we have final decisions or outcomes that don't look good for us, all because we have the *joyful anticipation of expected outcome,* or HOPE!

Here is an easy way to remember just what hope is.

Honesty—see yourself from God's perspective. Come up with an honest appraisal of who you are and where you are. We can only honestly appraise ourselves and our circumstances in light of God's truth: I AM God's child, 1 Peter 1:23, Galatians 4:7; I AM more than a conqueror, Romans 8:37; I AM beloved of God, Colossians 3:12, Romans 1:7; I AM set free, John 8:31–33; I AM blessed, Deuteronomy 28:1–14, Galatians 3:9. Apply God's truth and accept His love to activate HOPE.

Options—don't feel stuck. Hope is the key to life. My former pastor and friend, Dan Davis, in Austin, Texas, gave us a great book, *A Gift of Hope* by Robert Veninga. Therein are many illustrations of hope and hopelessness, and their ramifications. One illustration stood out to me: many elderly individuals entering a skilled-nursing facility were tracked based on whether they came to the facility voluntarily or involuntarily. The ones who entered the facility involuntarily passed away within several months. The ones who voluntarily entered the facility remained, for the most part, for several years. The point? When you see options, you see hope.

Review your options and pray for a plan. Seek advice from a pastor or mentor if you feel stuck. Proverbs 15:22 states, "Plans go wrong for lack of advice; many advisers bring success" (NLT).

Purpose/Plans—focus on the future. Read Jeremiah 29:11–14, which says God has plans, thoughts, and dreams for us. Then read Isaiah 43:18–19, which tells us to forsake the past and pursue the future, for God is doing a new thing. As a child of God, we have a God-given purpose, whether ministering to others or raising our children to follow the Lord. Obey His voice and get a plan—or let others help you formulate it.

Expectation—"I *can do* all things through Christ who strengthens me" (Philippians 4:13). Paul's expectation was to do all things through Christ. If we fear failure, we usually end up failing. Our minds and hearts have to be consumed with what we have in Christ, who is our strength, and not in our circumstances. Hope says, "I can!" Faith says, "I will!"

As we have read in previous chapters, Glenn Cunningham's mother believed more in God's report than in the doctor's prognosis. Wilma Rudolf believed more in her dad's encouragement to walk the aisle of a church than the doctor who said she couldn't. Henry Ford had confidence in his idea of an automated assembly line, even after five failed attempts. Thomas Edison's reply to a reporter who questioned why he continued to work toward the invention of the light bulb after so many failures was that he believed he was close because he was running out of ideas that didn't work. Beethoven created his famous Fifth Symphony while deaf. Elvis continued to play and sing even after the manager of the Grand Ole Opry told him to quit for lack of talent. Queen Esther worked a plan to free her people, even though she knew if she failed, she would die. Fifty-six men signed the Declaration of Independence knowing that if America failed, they would be hanged as traitors to England. *These stories and thousands of others never would have happened if they had let their failures and difficulties destroy their dreams.*

Hope is the joyful anticipation of expected outcome.

Think about It

1. What is the definition of hope?

2. Why is hope key to living?

3. What does the acronym HOPE stand for?

   H
   O
   P
   E

CHAPTER 10
Pushing Through the Pain Barrier

*But Daniel **purposed in his heart** that he would not defile*
himself with the portion of the king's delicacies.
—Daniel 1:8

I went to high school in San Jose, California, and swam in the same swim league as Mark Spitz. Mark was an incredible swimmer in high school and later went on to win seven gold medals in the 1972 Olympic Games in Germany.

Mark attended Santa Clara High School, and I was across town at Lynbrook High School. Swimming against the Santa Clara swim team was always a challenge, because we mostly saw the bottoms of their feet. There were several world-record holders on that team, of which Mark held five. A few years after retiring from swimming, I heard him comment on his years as a swimmer and what led to his incredible swimming records that stood for about forty years. He mentioned that he learned to swim at a young age in Honolulu, Hawaii, while on vacation with his parents. Soon after, he began swimming competitively in Chicago. During his junior-high years, the family moved to San Jose, California, to take advantage of the positive business environment and climate.

While Mark was well coached and won many swimming meets, he discovered something early on. In every race, there was a point where his muscles felt like they were on fire and where he felt he could go no further. He called that place the *pain barrier*. It was at this point a decision had to be made: to allow the pain barrier to slow him down or to push through the pain barrier toward victory. For Mark, the rewards of winning were great enough to keep him pushing through the pain. He said that the barrier was there in every race but that he "purposed in his heart" to push through it, and in each subsequent race, that choice became easier.

After I heard Mark's comments, I reflected on Daniel 1:8. Daniel had been torn from his family, his country, his traditions, and his language, but he stuck to his convictions when tempted. Daniel said he "purposed in his heart" not to defile his conscience. Daniel pushed through the pain barrier and eventually became the second in command in the Babylonian Empire. We all have some type of pain barrier somewhere in the pool of our lives. There is something we all must push through in order to become what our dreams hold for us.

Bob, the owner of Ironwood Ranch in Stewartville, Minnesota, and a graduate of the college I attended, suffered from a heavy-equipment accident in his early twenties that left him paralyzed from the waist down. Though confined to a wheelchair, Bob did not let the tragedy hold him back from pursuing his dreams; he just came up with new ones—like wheelchair racing and entering the Boston Marathon. He recalled the hardest part of the race at mile 18, heading up Heartbreak Hill. His arms were on fire, and he felt like he couldn't go on. He noticed that some of the runners had slowed down in order to make it up the hill, but he didn't have that option because if he slowed down or stopped, he would end up rolling backward into the Boston Harbor. Everyone in the crowd was cheering for him and encouraging him to keep going. At that point, all he wanted was for someone to come out of the crowd, grab the wheelchair handles, and help push him up the hill, but that would have disqualified him. Bob reported that during the pain of this moment, he got a vision of the Lord urging him on. "Come on, Bob, I'm here, you can do it! Keep going; I'm helping you! You can make it!" As a result, with God's help, Bob pushed through the pain barrier and finished the famous twenty-six-mile race.

I personally have a wonderful example of what happens when you don't push through the pain barrier. Our swim team swam against a crosstown rival, and the coach put me in against the second-best four-hundred-meter swimmer in the world. The advantage that day was that their pool was a little cooler than normal, which meant that you could push yourself a little harder because your body wanted to stay warm. Well, it seemed to work that day for me—at least for a while.

To my own surprise, I managed to stay even with Terry for nearly half the race. My teammates had gathered on each end of the pool screaming for me to "Go, go, go!" I stayed up with Terry for over two hundred yards, and then as I approached my pain barrier, I got to thinking, "If I keep swimming at this pace, someone will have to take me out of the pool in a fish net." So I started to pace myself and got a good glimpse of Terry's feet as he pulled ahead. When the race was over, my coach asked me how I felt. I said, "Okay," and then he said, "Don't ever feel okay at the end of a race again. We can help you out of the pool, but I want you to give it everything you've got!" My coach himself carried out his passionate pursuit and won a gold medal in the 1960 Rome Olympics. But it is good advice for us all, and I have to thank him again.

A number of years later, I became more interested in golfing than swimming, and I had the chance to meet Jim Sheard, PhD, while I was teaching a class at Celebration Church. He is one of the authors of *Finishing the Course*', a collection of golfers' insights into the game of golf and its spiritual implications. In one chapter of the book, Jim reflects on PGA golfer Steve Jones, who had struggled with health issues and sustained several injuries in a dirt-bike accident. One of his fingers was damaged so badly it took three years before he could get back on tour. It would have been much easier for Steve to quit and gone to coaching, but he stuck with it, surgeries and all. Due to the injury, Steve had to devise a completely new and unconventional grip, but his persistence and determination paid off as he rejoined the PGA Tour, won tournaments, and enjoyed a successful end to his golfing career. When asked how he was able to push through his pain barriers, he stated what he had learned through his circumstances: "I needed to play golf one shot at a time. Your next shot is the most important shot you'll ever hit. You need to concentrate on what is in the moment, it doesn't matter what you just did" (Sheard & Armstrong). That is exactly what we need to do too.

Another great athlete who had much to overcome was Jackie Robinson, a famous baseball player in the mid-1940s. He suffered extreme humiliation while working to break the color barrier in major-league baseball. His impressive major-league career spanned ten years, included six World Series, six consecutive All-Star Games, a .349 batting average, an MLB Rookie of the Year Award in 1947, and a National League Most Valuable Player Award in 1949. He was also the first black player inducted into the Baseball Hall of Fame in 1962. So how did he do it? While enduring the pain of discrimination, insults, and harassment, Jackie pushed through by changing his attitude and demeanor. Instead of reacting with typical anger, he channeled his energy in the direction of setting new baseball records and initiating social change.

There are many examples in the Scriptures of those who pushed through their pain barrier to get to their dream or purpose, among whom Jesus is the chief. How was Jesus able to push through the pain and shame of the cross? He was so consumed with His love for the heavenly Father, and for us, that He focused more on the goal than on the pain of the cross. It was the vision of what was set before Him—the joyful plan of salvation (Hebrews 12:1–2) and the glory of heaven—that pushed him through the ultimate pain barrier.

> The reward of winning will help pull you through the pain barrier.

Think about It

1. Think of a time when you encountered a difficult situation and you pushed through the pain barrier. How were you able to push through the pain?

2. What does the phrase "he purposed in his heart" mean to you?

3. What is your passionate pursuit?

CHAPTER 11

Getting from Here to There

Trust in the LORD with all your heart, and lean not on your own understanding;
in all your ways acknowledge Him, and He shall direct your paths.
—Proverbs 3:5-6

We have examined our hopes, dreams, and difficulties throughout the course of this book, but even so, you might be wondering how you overcome where you have been and get to where you want to be. Getting from "here" to "there" is a process, but God's Word provides both remedies and directions to give you clarity in identifying where you are and how to get to where God wants you to be.

At one time or another, we all want to get to a better place. Our regrets and our fear of the future can paralyze us in the present and steal our joy. With that in mind, consider what Moses told the people of Israel as they were preparing to cross over the Jordan River into the Promised Land. The people had, for forty years, been freed *from* slavery in Egypt, but it took that long to be freed *to* enter the Promised Land.

So Moses goes through all the ceremonial law in Leviticus correlating to God's holiness and then takes us to Leviticus 26:9–13, which is a direct word from God. "For I will look on you favorably and make you fruitful, multiply you and confirm My covenant with you. You shall eat the old harvest, and *clear out the old because of the new*. I will set My tabernacle among you, and My soul shall not abhor you. I will walk among you and be your God, and you shall be My people. I am the LORD your God, who brought you out of the land of Egypt, that you should not be their slaves; I have broken the bands of your yoke and made you walk upright." In this passage, God gives the following promises and direction:

1. I am going to bless you (a covenantal confirmation).
2. I will clear out the old and get ready for the new.
3. I will set my dwelling place among you, and I will not despise you.
4. I will be your God and you will be my people.
5. I am the Lord who brought you out of the slavery of Egypt.
6. I have broken the shackles of your slavery so you can walk upright.

In other words, in today's world, through Christ, God has set you free from all that holds you back in order to pursue all that God has in store for you. You have no excuses. So are you prepared *for* the change? And are you willing and prepared *to* change? Because to move from where you are or where you've been to where you want to be will require change.

Jesus made an important proclamation in John 8:32. "And you shall know the truth, and the truth shall make you free." That freedom may include freedom from slavery or freedom to pursue your future. In John 8:36, He proclaimed, "Therefore if the Son makes you free, you shall be free indeed." You are set free to be what He has called you to be. Declare your freedom by God's grace, and the chains will be broken. All that is left is to run with confidence the race that is before you, knowing that Christ has already run the race (Hebrews 12:1, 2).

In Exodus 14, we see the children of Israel stopped at the Red Sea with the Egyptian army quickly pursuing them. The Israelites panicked and said they wanted to go back to Egypt. Moses said stand still and watch. But God said lift up your rod, stretch out your hand over the sea, and *move* forward. The only way to get from here to there is by moving forward. God is constantly pushing His people forward when the tendency is to retreat or stand in paralysis.

Some forty years later, in Deuteronomy 2, God told the Israelites that they had been wandering around in the wilderness long enough—it was now time to move north. Then He informed them that all the barriers that kept them from entering the Promised Land the first time would be there again but to move on through them!

The past is unfixable. If your past is filled with sin—get forgiveness and move on! If your past is filled with hurt and difficulty—forgive and move on! If your past is filled with fear and procrastination—get up and move on! In any and all cases, *move!*

Problems, difficulties, and resistance do not mean that God is against you. Joseph's difficulties were designed by God to accomplish good in the long run (Psalm 105: 17–21).

God sent Joseph.
Joseph was under stress until his dreams were fulfilled.
God tested Joseph's character.
Joseph was eventually set free.
Joseph was eventually blessed.
Joseph was eventually used to save his family, and the entire nation of Israel.

Maybe the problems you've faced are designed by God to develop your skills, refine your character, and prepare you to accomplish something important.

God is calling you to focus on the future. Your thoughts can get stuck in the past, but God's truths are the keys to set your body, mind, and spirit free. These truths are God's specific revelation to you. The truths or promises you claim through faithful obedience not only releases you from your past, but also opens the doors to new opportunities or healing.

A good friend and well-known realtor in the Twin Cities area for over twenty-five years named Jeff Scislow, was given a fatal medical diagnosis of aplastic anemia in 2001. The disease rapidly destroyed all his bone marrow and left him without the ability to produce blood cells. However, instead of letting the diagnosis rule him, Jeff went to the great Healer, Jesus, and believed His prognosis for life, not death. He did not deny he was seriously ill, but he did not accept ownership of the disease. Instead, he earnestly prayed for God's healing and accepted it as provided in the truth of God's Word. He located and memorized key healing Scriptures such as Mark 11:24, Isaiah 53:5, and Psalm 34:19, which says, "Many are the afflictions of the righteous, but the Lord delivers him out of them all. " Jeff persistently declared these Scriptures out loud while believing God would honor His promises by bringing healing in his life. Jeff also incorporated diet changes and a regimen of vitamin supplements. He continued to use the key of God's promises to unlock his prison of disease. Jeff never lost hope in God, and was miraculously healed as a result. He tells his incredible story of God's healing in his book, *Journey to a Miracle—When Faith Was the Only Cure.*

It seems like everyone is seeking a change. We want our circumstances to change, our finances to change, or our relationships to change, and we would prefer them to change without our involvement. Change seems to be one of the most feared words in our language. It is what we want, but we tend to resist the process. It is much like going to the dentist. We want our teeth to look and feel better, but we don't want to go through the necessary dental procedures. We can't have one without the other! Sometimes significant change will not take place until the pain of the status quo is greater than the pain of change.

In John Maxwell's book *Winning with People*, he recorded the following words written on the tomb of an Anglican bishop buried in Westminster Abbey. "When I was young and free my imagination had no limits. I dreamed of changing the world. As I grew older and wiser, I discovered the world would not change, so I shortened my sights somewhat and decided to change only my country but it, too, seemed immovable. As I grew in my twilight years, in one last desperate attempt, I settled for changing only my family, those closest to me, but alas, they would have none of it. And now as I lie on my deathbed, I suddenly realized: If I had only changed my self first, then by example I would have changed my family. From their inspiration and encouragement, I would then have been able to better my country and who knows, I may have even changed my world."

Sometimes *you* have to change, if you want to get from where you are to where you want to be. But it is hard to change! It is so much easier to quit than to persist! "You have to start with a dream. But that dream will become a reality only if you bridge the gap between intentions and actions by identifying a series of goals" (Maxwell, *Your Road Map for Success*).

Your dream determines your goals.
Your goals map out your actions.

Your actions create results.

And the results bring you success. (Maxwell)

So how do we change? First, we must determine the outcome we desire or the goal we want or need to achieve. Then we must allow Christ to change *us* and empower us to achieve those outcomes and goals.

Most likely, the first thing that has to change is your *heart*. You need new emotional drives and attachments in your life, and that means you need a new heart; Ezekiel 36:25–27 says, "I will give you a new heart and put a new spirit within you; I will take the heart of stone out of your flesh and give you a heart of flesh." When you make a new decision to follow Jesus, you get a new heart that gives you new desires. Psalm 37:4 states, "Delight yourself also in the Lord, and He shall give you the desires of your heart. " Second Corinthians 5:17 confirms, "Therefore, if anyone is in Christ, he is a new creation; old things have passed away, behold, all things have become new."

Once you have a new heart and new desires, you need to get your *mind* right (S. Scott). "Old habits die hard" and new ones can only come from being reprogrammed. According to Proverbs 23:7a, "For as he thinketh in his heart, so is he." What is your mind filled with? Truth or lies? Frustration or faith? Problems or solutions? Think on the positive, think on the Truth. Philippians 4:7–8 tells us what to think. "And the peace of God which passeth all understanding, shall keep your hearts and minds through Christ Jesus. Finally, brethren, whatsoever things are true, whatsoever things are honest, whatsoever things are just, whatsoever things are pure, whatsoever things are lovely, whatsoever things are of good report; if there be any virtue, and if there be any praise, think on these things."

How do you see yourself? Who you think you are is who you

will be. If you think you are worthless, you will be worthless, but if you think you are significant, you will accomplish significant things. One of our former neighbors had a great singing voice and studied music in college. His dream was to be employed by a church as a worship leader. He did eventually land a job in a church, but it was as the janitor instead of the worship leader. One day, while chatting with him, I sensed he was struggling with something. I asked him what was bothering him. He told me how he had been a janitor for many years but that being a janitor was not what he had planned to do with his life. I asked, "How do you see yourself?" He told me that everyone at church saw him as a janitor. I asked him again, "But who do you see yourself as, a janitor or worship leader?" He responded, "A worship leader." I then gave him a statement from the movie, *The Last Starfighter*, when the main character says to a recruiter, "I'm just a kid from a trailer park." In the movie, the recruiter responds with, "If that's all you see, that's all you will ever be."

The conversation got my neighbor thinking and praying about his dream. A short time later, he made the decision to go back to school to get a master's degree in music. He and his wife sold their house and moved to another state where he could pursue his dream. A couple of years ago, I happened to be watching a church service on TV with an audience of thousands, and guess who the worship leader was. Yep—my neighbor, the janitor turned worship leader!

When your heart is right and you are thinking on the truth, your eyes (focus) then need to be locked on the new thing God is doing. Getting focused will bring your *priorities* in order (Canfield, Hansen, & Hewitt, *The Power of Focus*). So first focus on your heavenly purpose and then focus on what you do best. Use these questions found in *The Power of Focus* to define what you do best.

1. What do you do effortlessly?
2. What do you do that others find difficult?
3. What opportunities exist in the marketplace to utilize your best abilities and attributes?
4. What could you create using your unique talents?

Then move toward the open doors God provides.

The next thing to consider is what are you *saying*? We have talked about what fills your heart, *fills your mind,* and *fills your eyes* (focus), so now let's look at *what fills your mouth.* Psalm 19:14 says, "Let the words of my mouth and the meditation of my heart be acceptable in Your sight, O Lord my strength and my Redeemer." Jesus tells us in Matthew 17:20, "…if you have faith as a mustard seed, you will say to this mountain, 'Move from here to there' and it will move; and nothing will be impossible for you."

Our words can bring life or death, joy or sadness. The old chant, "sticks and stones may break my bones, but words will never hurt me," is absolutely untrue. Our words are powerful. Use them wisely to bring life, not death, to the situations you are in and to yourself.

So where are you headed right now? James 1:22 says, "But be doers of the word, and not hearers only deceiving yourselves." It does no good to only *know, believe,* and *think* what is right; we must also *do* what is right! That is faith—like Indiana Jones in *The Last Crusade* movie when he took the "step of faith" on an invisible path. We must not only believe in what may seem impossible, but also we must step out. This involves our feet. So start moving! According to Psalm 37:23, 24, "The steps of a good man are ordered by the Lord, and He delights in his way. Though he fall, he shall not be utterly cast down; for the Lord upholds him with his hand."

Do you really want to be free, and are you willing to do what it takes to become and remain free? If you are interested in getting from here to there and have been in your "here" for a long time, escaping could require making a drastic change, most likely an uncomfortable one. It will require different thoughts, attitudes, and actions. It may require getting help from someone like a pastor, counselor, or mentor, or it might require gaining additional education. But through God, all things are possible.

Take my brother, for instance. He had been struggling with his life over a three-to-four-year stretch after a divorce, the death of a close friend, and a severe motorcycle accident that required two surgeries to repair broken bones and put him into a long rehab program. Understandably, this left him very depressed, with too much time on his hands to think about negative things. When the divorce was taking place, he called to let us know and to ask for prayer. I had the opportunity to meet with him shortly after the motorcycle accident, and I could tell he was really questioning the choices he had made in life but felt stuck with no good options.

Becky and I began to pray diligently for him. We also requested our home Bible study group of fifteen to twenty folks to agree in prayer with us for him. Little did I realize, we would become the answer to our own prayers. About a year later, he called and stated things had spiraled down so low that he was in a dangerous place mentally. He didn't know what to do, and the alternatives were coming up short. He needed to get away from his situation. So, with our dad's help, he was able to leave where he was and come live with us in Minnesota. When I picked him up at the bus station downtown, he had all his earthly possessions in a duffle bag.

We didn't know what we were getting ourselves into, but the Lord had spoken to our hearts and told Becky and me to provide him a place to stay, offer him love, and give him space. I thought he might be more comfortable in the small church my son attends, so we connected him with that pastor. My brother loved to play guitar and write songs, so I loaned him my guitar. In a very short time, his life took an 180-degree turn. He surrendered his life to Christ and received a new blueprint for his life. He is now working at a church where he is greatly loved and appreciated. He got his own guitar and fulfilled a lifelong dream of recording a CD, and he is currently working on another. He plays and sings all over the Twin Cities and has been asked to share his testimony at different events and churches. He also holds a Bible study in our home once a week, and he has prayed for and counseled many people through their time of difficulty and grief. Wow! What a turnaround! It all started when he realized he needed a drastic change and said, "Help me." Then he found the keys in God's Word to unlock his shackles, and he was set free from his past. God did not use my brother's past against him but gave him a new present, and hope in the future.

How about you? You know you need to change. You would even like to change. But change is difficult and painful.

First, you must believe you can and will change. When we make up our mind to change, we can do it with God's help. A principle I learned from my diving coach was that the body will always follow your head. To stop the rotation of your body while diving, you have to pull your head up. To start the rotation of your body during a dive, you have to spin your head in the direction you want your body to rotate. It's the same with change. When our minds change, our bodies will follow. In other words, agree with God's truth, step out in faith, and change will come.

Be aware that the enemy of your soul, Satan, does not want you to better yourself or your situation, so he will launch obstacles to distract and derail you. The struggle will get harder, and the key to unlocking your shackles might be elusive. Your decisions will become more critical the closer you come to the dream you strive for. So if you find yourself in an intense struggle, you just might be at the goal line!

God, our heavenly Father, who loves and works with us individually, gives us His truth. When we apply His truth to our situations, and believe and obey it, it becomes the key to unlocking the prison of our circumstances.

There are a lot of people who are haunted by their pasts, but when the chains of the past are broken, we are free *to* pursue plans for the future and look forward to the new thing God has for us! Embrace the new thing He is bringing your way, and you will be on the right path to getting from here to there and *Defining Life by Your Dreams Not Difficulties.*

Significant change will not take place until the pain of the status quo is greater than the pain of change.

Think about It

1. What have you been set free from and set free to?

2. What is one area in your life that needs change? Make a plan and get started!

3. Keep a journal of God's blessings and answered prayers.

References and Resources

"9 Things Invented or Discovered by Accident." *How Stuff Works.* http://science.howstuffworks.com/innovation/scientific-experiments/9-things-invented-or-discovered-by-accident4.htm#page=9

Bardwell, Bob. http://www.ironwoodsprings.com/bobbardwell.aspx

Bethel, S. M. *Making a Difference: 12 Qualities That Make You a Leader.* New York: The Berkley Publishing Group, 1990.

Canfield, Jack, Mark Victor Hansen, and Les Hewitt. *The Power of FOCUS.* Deerfield Beach, FL: Health Communication Inc., 2000.

Carlson, Dwight, and Susan Carlson Wood. *When Life Isn't Fair.* Eugene, OR: Harvest House, 1989.

Colson, Chuck. http://www.who2.com/bio/chuck-colson

Colonel Sanders biography. http://www.biography.com/people/colonel-harland-sanders-12353545#synopsis

Crouch, A. "Through It All." http://www.lyricsmania.com/through_it_all_lyrics_andrae_crouch.html

Dave Dravecky. http://www.davedravecky.com/index.cfm/PageID/862/index.html and interview found at https://www.youtube.com/watch?v=HQMhUlFka0w

Dickens, C. *A Tale of Two Cities*. http://www.online-literature.com/dickens/twocities/1/

Don't Quit. http://www.usdreams.com/DontQuit172.html

Eker, T. H. *Secrets of the Millionaire Mind*. New York: Harper Collins Publishers, 2005.

Elvis Presley. http://www.rainbeforerainbows.com/presley.html and http://theboot.com/elvis-presley-grand-ole-opry/

Glenn Cunningham. http://bleacherreport.com/articles/198249-forgotten-stories-of-courage-and-inspiration-glenn-cunningham

Henry Ford. http://www.tmgenealogy.com/2012/10/henry-ford-10-fun-facts-businessman.html and http://www.goodreads.com/author/quotes/203714.Henry_Ford

HOLY BIBLE. New American Standard Bible. Chicago: Moody Publishers, 1977.

HOLY BIBLE. All scriptures from the New King James Version unless otherwise noted. Nashville: Thomas Nelson Publishers, Inc., 1982.

HOLY BIBLE. New Living Translation. Wheaton: Tyndale House Publishers, Inc., 1996.

Kurt Warner biography. http://www.biography.com/people/ kurt-warner-519490#synopsis and https://www.youtube. com/watch?v=48PJbdjM-GE interview

Lucado, M. *Six Hours One Friday*. Sisters: Multnomah Books, 1989.

MacDonald, G. *Ordering Your Private World*. Nashville: Thomas Nelson Publishers, 2003.

Mandino, O. *Og Mandino's University of Success*. New York: Bantam Books, 1982.

Maxwell, J. C. *Your Road Map for Success*. Nashville: Thomas Nelson, 2002.

Maxwell, J. C. *Winning with People*. Nashville: Thomas Nelson, 2004.

McLaughlin, Billy. Billy McLaughlin biography. http://www. billymclaughlin.com/biography/ and interview used by permission

McPherson, Matt, and Sherry McPherson. "The Salvation Poem." http://thesalvationpoem.com/#chapter_2 . Used by permission.

Peters, Tom, and Robert Waterman. *In Search of Excellence*. New York: HarperCollins Publisher, 1982.

Rocky Marciano's Greatest Fights: Marciano-Walcott. http://sports.espn.go.com/sports/boxing/news/story?id=2481103 and Ring Magazine, December 1952

Schuller, R. H. *Tough Times Never Last, But Tough People Do.* New York: Bantam Books, 1984.

Scislow, J. *Journey to a Miracle.* Fort Collins: A Book's Mind, 2014.

Scott, S. K. *Simple Steps to Impossible Dreams.* New York: Fireside, 1998.

Sheard, Jim, and Wally Armstrong. *Finishing the Course.* Nashville: J. Countryman, 2000.

Swindoll, C. "Attitudes." Copyright © 1981, 1982 by Charles R. Swindoll, Inc. All rights reserved worldwide. Used by permission.

The Oakland Press. (December 14, 2010). Long-lost painting worth $1M at Detroit Institute of Arts. www.theoaklandpress.com/ ... /long-lost-painting-worth ...

Theodore Roosevelt quote. http://www.brainyquote.com/quotes/quotes/t/theodorero403358.html#IWQ7BtOU1oDqbHe3.99

Thomas Edison. http://www.manythings.org/voa/people/Thomas_Edison.html and http://www.brainyquote.com/quotes/authors/t/thomas_a_edison.html

Tracy, B. *Maximum Achievement*. New York: Simon & Schuster, 1993.

Veninga, R. L. *A Gift of Hope*. New York: Ballantine Books, 1985.

Walt Disney. http://www.businessinsider.com/successful-people-who-failed-at-first-2014-3?op=1 and http://www.hiddenmickeys.org/secrets/walt.html

Washington, B. T. *Up from Slavery*. http://docsouth.unc.edu/fpn/washington/washing.html

Wilma Rudolph. http://www.manythings.org/voa/people/Wilma_Rudolph.html and http://www.biography.com/people/wilma-rudolph-9466552#early-life

Ziglar, Z. *See You at the Top*. Gretna: Pelican Publishing Company, 1975.

Zschech, D. Hillsong's Darlene Zschech on "How I wrote "Shout to the Lord"". https://www.youtube.com/watch?v=20kP79XJox4

About the Authors

George and Becky Gilmour have been teaching and ministering in local churches since they were teenagers. They met in Bible college, were married, and have been partners in ministry for more than forty years. George earned a degree in Bible and history from Pacific Coast Baptist Bible College and is currently credentialed for pastoral ministry through International Ministerial Fellowship. George and Becky have worked in local churches in a variety of capacities, from teens to senior adults. The Gilmours experienced a parent's worst nightmare in 1981 when their four-year-old daughter was killed in a traffic accident. Through this tragedy, they experienced God's overwhelming love and learned firsthand the real meaning of hope. For the past thirty years, they have been dispensing hope through their seminar ("Navigating through the Storms of Life"), *Drive Time Inspiration* CD, and one-on-one counseling. They currently live in Burnsville, Minnesota. They have two married sons: Chad and his wife, Danielle; and Jason and his wife Joanna, who have four beautiful daughters named Amara, Rayna, Bailey, and Evelyn. The Gilmours also have an affectionate golden retriever named Buddy.

The Gilmours are available for speaking engagements. Contact them via email at: defininglife2@gmail.com

Acknowledgments

I am forever grateful for the following people God strategically placed in my life at just the right time.

Thank You, Jesus, for loving even me and being with us through the storms of life. Thank You for entrusting us with this story that You wanted told!

I thank the late Dr. David Laurie of Trinity Baptist Church in Sunnyvale, California, who many years ago introduced me to Christ and the grace of God by living it and sharing it. He always used to say, "It's not our job to see through one another, but just to see one another through." That is the essence of the Golden Rule.

On earth, there is no one to whom I am more thankful than my wife, Becky. I took her off a farm in Minnesota to a thriving metropolis in Southern California in 1974. The time there was like *A Tale of Two Cities*—it was the best of times, it was the worst of times. We both experienced this book and God's working in our lives. I am so thankful for her ability to take my rambling and wordsmith it into something readable! You are the love of my life, and I am forever grateful God brought us together.

I thank my dear friend, Dr. Dan Davidson, under whom I served as associate pastor of Anaheim Baptist Church and who mentored me in ministry. I also thank the people of Anaheim Baptist who helped us through the hardest day of our lives.

I thank Pastor Dan Davis of Hope Chapel in Austin, Texas, who helped us with the next leg of our spiritual journey. Through his preaching and personal ministry to us, he unwittingly contributed to a lot of material in this book.

I thank Rev. Larry and Judy Frick who allowed us to compile and first teach this material at their church in Farmington, Minnesota.

I also thank the evangelist Pastor Lowell Lundstrom, Pastor Londa Lundstrom Ramsey, and Pastor Rob Ketterling for their input through the preaching of God's truth and contributing to our spiritual growth.

I thank our great friends in Austin, Texas, Ron and Sandy Winn, Brian and Ruth Catalano, and Ralph and Billie Korstad for being the kind of friends that pushed us closer to Jesus and helped us recover from our tragic loss.

I thank our current Lifegroup friends (you know who you are) who are great prayer warriors and encouragers to our ministry. Also, my dear friend Heath, who taught me two very important lessons. After his son's accidental death, he mentioned that people had told him that life was not fair. In response, he told them that in fact life was fair; it was just indiscriminant. (The rain and drought come to the righteous and unrighteous). He also said that if you ever see a turtle sitting on a fence post, you know it had help getting there. Thanks, Heath. I am one of those turtles.

A special thanks to Tom Gonsor, Amway Diamond, for his suggestion to include a practical "How to" chapter. Consequently, the final chapter "Getting from Here to There" was born.

A huge thank you to Brennan McPherson for your expertise

in editing this book. You were able to really "get" what we were trying to say and helped us say it so much better. Your edits made a huge difference!

A final thank you to our sons, Jason and Chad. Thank you, Jason, for designing the book cover and adding your photography talent to this project. Thank you, Chad, for adding your professional touch to our photo and giving us project advice! You guys are the best, and we are so blessed to have your help with this project!

CPSIA information can be obtained
at www.ICGtesting.com
Printed in the USA
JSHW012032271122
33791JS00002B/5